*i*MONEY

*i*MONEY

Profitable ETF Strategies
for Every Investor

TOM LYDON
JOHN F. WASIK

Vice President, Publisher: Tim Moore
Associate Publisher and Director of Marketing: Amy Neidlinger
Executive Editor: Jim Boyd
Operations Manager: Gina Kanouse
Development Editor: Russ Hall
Digital Marketing Manager: Julie Phifer
Publicity Manager: Laura Czaja
Assistant Marketing Manager: Megan Colvin
Marketing Assistant: Brandon Smith
Cover Designer: Chuti Prasertsith
Managing Editor: Kristy Hart
Copy Editor: Krista Hansing Editorial Services, Inc.
Indexer: Cheryl Lenser
Compositor: Jake McFarland
Manufacturing Buyer: Dan Uhrig

© 2008 by Pearson Education, Inc.
Publishing as FT Press
Upper Saddle River, New Jersey 07458

FT Press offers excellent discounts on this book when ordered in quantity for bulk purchases or special sales. For more information, please contact U.S. Corporate and Government Sales, 1-800-382-3419, corpsales@pearsontechgroup.com. For sales outside the U.S., please contact International Sales at international@pearson.com.

Company and product names mentioned herein are the trademarks or registered trademarks of their respective owners.

Printed in the United States of America

First Printing June 2008

ISBN-10: 0-13-712739-1
ISBN-13: 978-0-13-712739-9

Pearson Education LTD.
Pearson Education Australia PTY, Limited.
Pearson Education Singapore, Pte. Ltd.
Pearson Education North Asia, Ltd.
Pearson Education Canada, Ltd.
Pearson Educatión de Mexico, S.A. de C.V.
Pearson Education—Japan
Pearson Education Malaysia, Pte. Ltd.

Library of Congress Cataloging-in-Publication Data

Lydon, Tom, 1960-
    iMoney : profitable etf strategies for every investor / Tom Lydon,
John F. Wasik.
        p. cm.
    Includes bibliographical references and index.
    ISBN 0-13-712739-1 (hardback : alk. paper) 1. Exchange traded funds. 2. Portfolio management. 3. Investments. I. Wasik, John F. II. Title. III. Title: Building wealth with exchange traded funds.
    HG6043.L93 2008
    332.63'27—dc22
                                2008001143

Thanks to Mom and Dad and to my wife, Lisa Ann
and our kids, Creagan, Cameron, and Anya,
for their love and support

—Tom

To Julia Theresa

—JW

Contents

Acknowledgments

Acknowledgments for Tom Lydon

I'd like to thank the numerous people who generously gave us their time and shared their thoughts about ETFs, including the many readers of ETFTrends.com and fellow investment advisors, whose ideas, feedback, and opinions are what made this book possible.

Friends in the ETF industry: Darwin Abrahamson, David Blitzer, Bobby Brooks, Dennis Clark, Lisa Dallmer, Dan Dolan, Jeff Feldman, Don Friedman, Gary Gastineau, Jim Guilfoil, Jeremy Held, Bob Holderith, Kevin Ireland, Christian Magoon, Tim Meyer, Adam Phillips, Kevin Rich, Tony Rochte, Jim Ross, Steve Sachs, Jeremy Siegel, and Sam Stovall.

Fellow writers, bloggers, investors, and friends in the financial media: Eileen Ambrose, Tom Anderson, Sue Asci, Jeannine Aversa, Russell Bailyn, Maria Bartiromo, Heather Bell, Stephen Bernard, Jonathon Bernstein, David Bogoslaw, Kurt Bower, Alan Brochstein, Sean Brodrick, Veronica Brown, Joe Bel Bruno, Kevin Burke, Mike Burnick, Scott Burns, Barry Burr, Jonathon Burton, Dan Caplinger, Lawrence Carrel, Larry Carroll, Rob Carrick, Shu-Ching Jean Chen, Stan Choe, Nicola Clark, Jonathan Clements, Murray Coleman, Larry Connell, Simon Constable, Glenn Curtis, Martin Crutsinger, Carl Delfeld, Don Dion, Ryan J. Donmoyer, Bill Donoghue, Rich Duprey, Tate Dwinnel, Lee Edgcomb, Jesse Emspak, Paul B. Farrell, Jackie Farwell, Rick Ferri, Mark Fightmaster, Randall Forsyth, Melissa Francis, Doris Frankel, Dave Fry, Peter Garnham, Cardiff de Alejo Garcia, David Gonzalez, Prashant Gopal, Gary Gordon, Bob Grayson, Diya Gullapalli, Sara Hansard, Steve Hargreaves, Daniel Harrison, Ray Hendon, Arthur B. Hill, Roger Hing, Trang Ho, David Hoffman, Eli Hoffmann, Matt Hougan, Chuck Jaffe, Mark Jewell, Richard Kang, David Kathman, Rob Kelley, John Kenchington, Kevin Kennedy, Ted Kennedy, Donald J. Korn, Matt Krantz, Reinhardt Krause, Michael Krauss, George D. Lambert, Paul R. La Monica, Mike Larson, Tom

Lawrence, Rob Lenihan, Polya Lesova, Jennifer Levitz, Jim Lowell, Aaron Lucchetti, Michael Maiello, Andy Mayo, Matthew D. McCall, Will McClatchy, Suzanne McGee, Peter McKay, Daniel McNulty, Andrew Mickey, David Mildenberg, Dave Mock, Brian Moore, Joe Morris, Greg Newton, Ulli G. Niemann, Roger Nusbaum, Tim Paradis, Nick Passmore, Nick Perry, James Picerno, Jeff Pietsch, Bob Pisani, Prieur du Plessis, Michael A. Pollock, Robin Pomeroy, Brian Powers, Atul Prakash, Jeffrey Ptak, Vito J. Racanelli, Madlen Read, Laura Rowley, Frederic Ruffy, Tony Sagami, Ian Salisbury, David Schrader, Assif Shameen, Aaron Siegel, Bernard Simon, Evan Simonoff, David Smith, Donn Soderquist, John Spence, Brett Steenbarger, Ben Stein, Charlie Stroller, Asif Suria, Chan Tien Hin, Peter Tolk, Walter Updegrave, Zoe Van Schnydel, Alex Veiga, Joanne Von Alroth, Richard Waters, Martin Weiss, Charles Wheelan, Rob Wherry, Rich White, Jim Wiandt, John Wilen, Leslie Wines, David Winning, Greg Wolper, Shirley Won, and Wanfeng Zhou.

I'd like to thank Kate Luce, Michael Thomsett, and Russ Hall for their editing prowess; Jim Boyd, Kristy Hart, and Julie Phifer at Prentice Hall for taking us on and guiding us; and John Wasik for his partnership, hard work, and expertise in our collaboration.

Thanks to Virginia Zart and Melody Harris for they day-to-day support and for putting up with me.

A special thank you to Heather Hayes for leading this project from start to finish. Her research, interviews, writing, and sense of humor made this loads of fun.

Finally, thanks to Mom and Dad and to my wife, Lisa Ann and our kids, Creagan, Cameron, and Anya, for their love and support.

Acknowledgments for John Wasik

I'd like to thank my patient wife, Kathleen, and my daughters, Sarah and Julia, for their enduring love and tolerance. It has also been a sincere pleasure working with Tom's diligent and thoughtful staff at Global Trends, particularly Heather and Virginia. And to all my respected colleagues at Bloomberg News, thanks for your supreme professionalism.

About the Authors

Tom Lydon is the editor of ETFTrends.com and the president of Global Trends Investments. He has been involved in money management for more than 20 years. He began his career with Fidelity Investments' Institutional Division. He now regularly appears on CNBC's "ETF Tracker," a daily segment focusing on ETFs. His popular seminar, "How to Manage a Million-Dollar Portfolio," has been attended by thousands of investors around the country. Mr. Lydon holds a bachelor of science in management from Babson College in Wellesley, Massachusetts.

John F. Wasik is the award-winning personal finance columnist for Bloomberg News, the world's third-largest news service. His columns are seen by readers on five continents and posted on www.bloomberg.com. As the author of ten books, including the highly praised *Merchant of Power* and *The Bear-Proof Investor*, he has spoken from coast to coast. He earned his bachelor and master of arts degrees from the University of Illinois–Chicago and resides in Grayslake, Illinois, with his wife and two children. Visit him online at www.johnwasik.com.

Preface

ETFs for Everyone

Time and research have demonstrated that individual investors like you want to be empowered—and to get there, you are seeking new information, new products, and more powerful tools to aid in your quest. You want control over your portfolio, and you want to know what's actually in it. Thanks to great advances in technology and the increasing globalization of the world economy, today it's easier than ever for you to take investments into your own hands.

Maybe you already know about exchange traded funds (ETFs), but you'd like to know more. Or you know a lot about them, but you haven't quite figured out how to incorporate them into your portfolio. With hundreds of ETFs dotting the financial landscape, becoming ever more specialized and covering some creatively constructed indexes, trying to figure out how they work and how to use them to your best advantage can be a daunting task.

We've taken the time to speak with and e-mail individual investors just like you. We've actively solicited your comments and input on our blog, ETFTrends.com, every step of the way. We asked: How did you discover ETFs? What have your experiences been so far? And how do you use them to your advantage? Your answers helped shape the direction of this book. We also sought expert advice and opinions about ETFs—where they've been and where they're going. We've done extensive research, in an attempt to make this book the one-stop-shop for ETF information. And we hope it will be light and entertaining as well.

ETFs came into existence in the early 1990s, but they didn't really take off until a series of scandals rocked the mutual fund industry. Today they're a formidable challenger to the mutual fund throne. To understand ETFs fully is to know where they came from and how they—and the underlying indexes they track—are created. This is why we've broken it down for you and given you a brief history before we dive in and discuss the nuts and bolts of the industry. We also have special chapters devoted to both buy-and-hold and trading strategies.

It's now more important than ever to ensure that you have a handle on your retirement savings. With lavish pension plans quickly becoming extinct, people can no longer just assume that the government will carry them through. How dire is the situation? During World War II, there were 42 workers paying into Social Security for each person receiving benefits. By 2030, projections are that only two working people will be contributing for each person receiving benefits—and most baby boomers will be retired by then. Ouch. But all is not lost if you firmly resolve to look out for yourself and your money.

Our goal in writing this book is to give you confidence to make wise, educated, and informed choices about the investments you make when it comes to ETFs. We want you to have a solid grasp of how ETFs work. You will be able to put together a portfolio that works best for you, and you'll have the tools to manage your portfolio effectively. Ultimately, we want you to be a successful investor.

—Tom Lydon

A Multipurpose Tool

ETFs are the Swiss Army knives of investments. They can do myriad things for millions, yet provide a single tool that's extremely specialized. Over 20 years and in 5 books on investing, I've yearned for such a tool. Now that ETFs have entered the mainstream, it's finally possible for everyone to start using them to boost their returns and lower their investment costs.

I've long been troubled by high expenses and lack of transparency in annuities, brokerage accounts, mutual funds, and retirement plans. Do you know how much brokers, middlemen, and fund managers are gouging you for investing your money? What about your 401(k) or pension fund? If you don't know, it's probably too much.

I've seen instances of investors being fleeced for more than 3 percent per year in some accounts. I know that doesn't sound like much, but considering that an ETF offers the same range of investment products *and* much more diversification and transparency for as little as .07 percent per year, it should make you mad. It makes *me* mad every time I hear from one of my ripped-off readers.

Enter ETFs, which you can look into with fishbowl transparency, pay rock-bottom fees for, and track on stock exchanges every hour of the day. ETFs that invest in stock indexes offer you the added feature of lowering your tax bill. Because they hold a constant basket of stocks, they almost never generate capital gains taxes. In this sense, they are far more efficient than actively traded mutual funds. And because ETFs are mostly a static pool of securities, you don't have to suffer from managers making bad decisions—which they make consistently—in timing the market.

Why employ a manager or broker to guess on a single hot stock, sector, industry, or country? You don't have to because ETFs enable you to buy entire markets. Of course, even though they are a worthwhile tool to build wealth, they are far from perfect; you need to know how to use them. That way, you'll be able to take charge of your investments and reach all of your financial goals. You'll also achieve what I call a "New Prosperity"—that is, the point at which your investments serve you silently so that you're free to live the life you want.

The core of the iMoney philosophy is that you put *information*— the *i* in *iMoney*—to work to create knowledge. We'll help you avoid powerful yet consistent pitfalls in investing, to use the current information available at ETFTrends.com and other resources, and other investment research to convert your newfound knowledge into wisdom that you'll be able to use the rest of your life. We've taken the best ideas from investment savants such as Jack Bogle, Warren Buffett, Burton Malkiel, and others to help you craft flexible, customized portfolios that work for you over time. Along the way, we've sampled the wisdom of Modern Portfolio Theory, behavioral finance, and Nobel Prize–winning economists to make the learning curve less steep.

Better yet, by employing our iMoney strategies, you won't be able to blame someone else for taking advantage of you. As the old maxim goes, "Only a bad carpenter blames his tools." Read, enjoy, and prosper.

—John F. Wasik

Introduction: A New Investment Strategy

I always said that no one will look out for your money better than you. Nobody cares as much as I do.

—Kentucky investor Donn Soderquist

In the late 1960s, Tom's dad was a stockbroker in Boston and he recalls fondly that his office was on one of the top floors of the Prudential Building, which at the time was the tallest building in the city. When he took me to the office, I was impressed with not just all the machines, ticker tape, and phones, but also the fact that my dad's company literally towered above all of the other companies in the Boston area.

Seeing that sparked an interest in what my dad actually did. He explained that he helped people manage their money, and he taught me a little about companies and stocks. As I learned more, I asked my dad where he invested his money, and he said, "Mutual funds."

Dad liked to read *Barron's* on the weekends, and back in the 1960s, you had to have a copy reserved at your local store. Many Saturdays, we'd take a drive into the next town to pick up the latest issue. In the middle of each magazine were pages of statistical information on individual stocks. One small section on a single page listed the 300 to 400 mutual funds that were available at the time.

Dad explained to me the advantages funds had over stocks (they were diversified) and said that instead of owning individual stocks, you could hold a basket of stocks. Theoretically, if the general market went up, the mutual fund would go up as well. If you bought an individual stock, it wasn't always guaranteed that if the market moved up, the stock would. As time went on and my interest grew, I'd grab Dad's copy of *Barron's* and look to see how his Nicholas Fund was doing.

Over the years, I enjoyed continuing my education about mutual funds as their popularity grew, the number of fund companies grew, and the number of mutual funds grew. After I graduated from college, I interviewed with Fidelity Institutional. One of the main interview questions was, "Can you tell us what a mutual fund is?" Although I had gone to an undergraduate college that's known for its business program, we spent very little time actually learning about investments. If I hadn't spent the time with my dad learning the ins and outs of mutual funds and thumbing through his copy of *Barron's*, I would have surely messed up that interview.

Investors Want More

The growth of the Exchange Traded Funds (ETF) marketplace reminds me of the growth of mutual funds in the late 1960s, 70s and 80s. Investors are still looking for diversified investment options run by qualified individuals who worked at trusted companies with big names.

Over the past few decades, trillions of dollars have flowed into the mutual fund arena, and for the most part, investors have been served well. But today they are looking for more. *You want diversification, and you need to know exactly what managers are buying. And you're more price conscious than ever.*

With today's advances in technology and communication, individual investors and advisors desire a more active role in directing their portfolios. Not all investors feel the need to pay a fund manager to make the decisions for buying and selling for a particular mutual fund. Instead, they tend to appreciate the flexibility of being able to select asset classes, sectors, or global regions in a quick, easy, efficient, and inexpensive way.

Sure, those conventional mutual funds will continue to proliferate. But ETFs are on the verge of hitting a tipping point in the eyes of individual investors and financial advisors as a greater percentage of new money flows into ETFs.

Just a few decades ago, only a few hundred mutual funds existed. But when they really caught on with the general populace, they took off so quickly that they made the Road Runner look pokey. After several years of holding steady in their numbers—a few hundred or so—new funds suddenly began appearing almost daily by the late 1970s. It was as though someone had found a mutual fund dandelion and blew the seeds this way and that. Funds were on fire, and their managers were stars.

Mutual funds covered it all—all asset classes, sectors, and global regions. There were mutual funds covering almost any area a big-thinking investor could dream up—it was simply a matter of putting together a basket of stocks. At the height of it all, it must have been a nightmare for a person who has trouble making decisions, with 11,000 mutual funds to choose from.

Although the number of mutual funds has declined in recent years because of the wounded trust resulting from scandals of the late 1990s and growing investor education about their shortcomings, they still have longevity and name recognition. They're like your favorite slippers—a little beat up, but still cozy and familiar. They won't be going anywhere anytime soon, and, if nothing else, mutual funds have proved the naysayers wrong. They did become big, and they are sticking around.

The mutual fund industry became an unqualified success story, with more than $24 trillion in assets worldwide. It now has a worthy rival.

Enter the ETF, the Younger, Sleeker Cousin of the Mutual Fund

Much like mutual funds during their rapid growth period, ETFs are sprouting up like June corn in an Iowa field. After hitting the market in 1992, ETFs now hold nearly $600 billion in assets in more than 600 funds. Considering that only 32 funds were trading in 1999, representing only $36 billion, their ascent has been dramatic. By comparison, the mutual fund industry, which began in 1924, took 60 years to reach the same asset level that ETFs enjoy today. The exchange traded fund market is expected to grow 33 percent annually until 2010, reaching almost $2 trillion.

Some days several new ETFs come to market. And if there isn't an existing index—say, something for a particular country or currency—ETF providers will go ahead and create an index and build an ETF around it if there's enough interest. Although the first—and, by far, the most popular—ETFs were the traditional ones that track stock indexes, an ever-growing variety of ETFs covers specialized sectors and markets (stocks, currencies, commodities). Chances are, you could find an ETF that seems as though it was tailor made for you. And much like the mutual funds did when they were proliferating, new ETFs are appearing all the time from a combination of factors—chiefly, consumer demand and whatever is the latest, hottest sector.

ETFs are the brash new kid on the block, offering innovation and a stream of fresh ideas. They're turning a decades-old formula on its head, offering greater flexibility, more opportunities for diversification, and the chance for investors to get in on exciting markets that were previously closed to them. Here's what they are and what they do better than mutual funds:

- **They're served up in a basket.** Like mutual funds, ETFs pool various securities—stocks, bonds, commodities, currencies—into one package. Most often these packets are reflected by an index that represents a large group of investments. The Standard & Poor's 500 index represents the 500 largest stocks by market value, for example. This basket is then treated like an individual security and listed on an exchange. Constantly creating and redeeming shares "in-kind," ETFs exchange shares for pools of underlying securities.

- **They make trading easy.** As separate, listed securities, ETFs trade just like stocks. You can buy and sell them through brokers, and they are traded throughout the day. Their prices constantly reflect changes in market prices. They are different from open-ended mutual funds, in which investors buy shares in a pool of securities. Mutual funds are not listed on exchanges. When you purchase shares in an open-ended mutual fund, new shares are created. With ETFs, you buy them the same way you would a stock, using techniques such as shorting (selling in anticipation of a price drop), limit-buys, and stop-loss orders. You can also write options—both calls and puts—against ETFs. You can't do that with mutual funds.

- **You know what you're buying.** ETF managers publish their holdings every day and note any changes. Most portfolios that represent an index rarely change at all. You know what you own at all times. What you see is what you get. That's not possible with an open-end, actively traded mutual fund, which only has to publish quarterly statements and won't fully disclose its trading expenses. As such, ETFs are not subject to the kind of trading abuses that have ravaged mutual funds in the last decade. ETFs are continuously repriced throughout the trading day, so late trading isn't possible. In comparison, the net asset value (NAV) of traditional mutual funds is always a trading day's closing price.

- **Their cost is very low.** Because there's little in the way of trading costs—holdings in index ETFs are rarely sold—management fees are low. Although you'll pay a brokerage commission to buy or sell them (we recommend working with a deep-discount broker), expenses are minimal in ETFs because they are efficient. Considering that the average actively managed stock mutual fund charges you 1.50 percent per year in management expenses, the savings are significant, according to Morningstar, Inc., the Chicago-based financial information company. The average U.S. stock ETF charges .41 percent annually.

- **They're tax friendly.** If an actively managed, open-end mutual fund has a good year, you'll often pay for it in taxable gains outside of a tax-deferred account. Not so in most ETFs, which are largely insulated from the need to sell holdings for shareholder redemptions. Most index ETFs have static portfolios that are passively managed, so they generate gains only if a security needs to be sold because the index keepers have changed the index. So most ETFs don't generate capital gains from buying and selling components; you pay tax only on profits from selling your ETF shares, meaning that you also control the timing of taxable outcomes.

- **They help you diversify and reduce risk.** Because ETFs are broad baskets of securities, they can represent entire markets. Want to buy a fund representing all listed U.S. or foreign stocks? How about sampling most large overseas stocks? Or U.S. bonds? ETFs can do that and more. By giving you exposure to more securities, they lower your portfolio risk. You need never buy another single stock or actively managed mutual fund again. Why gamble far too much money on what you think will be the next Google when you can buy an entire fund full of potential winners from all over the world?

Profit with Prudence, Avoid the Hype

ETFs are the good-looking new kid in school, the one the other students want to get to know a little better. Getting swept up in a lot of hype, though, could be deadly to the money you're investing. ETFs may be a welcome addition to any portfolio, but they are hardly perfect. Unlike no-load mutual funds, you can't buy them directly from the distributor.

You need to purchase them through a broker, preferably a deep-discount house. And it may not make sense to buy them in small increments because you will be dinged with a commission every time you buy or sell. If it costs you more than .50 percent per transaction, buying through a similar index mutual fund might make more sense if the ETF equivalent is available. If you do dollar-cost averaging by buying a small number of shares each month, ETFs may not be the right vehicle for you unless you're in a specialized plan that can buy shares through a trust or retirement plan (see Chapter 12, "iMoney ETF Portfolios"). If you want to generate dividend income from an ETF, make sure your broker pays those directly to you or allows for automatic dividend reinvestment.

Also keep in mind that because ETFs trade during the day, their NAV, or the total value of all securities held in the portfolio, also changes. There may be a slight difference between the NAV and the fund's market value, known as a premium or a discount. There's rarely a very large gap between the two numbers, although you should be aware that it exists.

The low management costs of ETFs also make them a little too appealing, so you might fall prey to the "buffet effect." When something is cheap, we tend to buy more of it, whether we need to or not. We know the temptations of a hot new product that promises unlimited wealth. Can you spell *dot.com*? As streamlined investment vehicles, ETFs strive to do what mutual funds have done, only with more investor-friendly features. Yet you can't fully take advantage of ETFs unless you understand what they are and what they can do. We hope to provide a roadmap to ETFs through our iMoney strategies.

How to Use This Book

The beautiful thing about ETFs is how you can tailor them to your goals and your ability to stomach portfolio risk. Are you a staunchly conservative buy-and-hold investor? We've got several portfolios that could work for you, just as we do for the daredevils among you who prefer lots of trading and a black diamond level of risk.

- If you know all you need to know about the history of ETFs, skip to Chapter 3, "Investing in Domestic Shares: U.S. Stock Index ETFs."

- Just need ideas for building your own portfolio? Chapter 12, "iMoney ETF Portfolios," offers you one-stop shopping.

- Want to take the plunge and explore the new world of commodity or currency investing? Go to Chapters 6, "Gold, Silver, and Oil: Commodity ETFs," and 7, "A Buck Isn't Worth a Dollar: Currency ETFs."

- Just want to build secure retirement portfolios? Sample Chapter 10, "Hedging Your Bets: Long and Short ETFs."

- Don't have a clue about ETFs? If you're just getting started, go to the next chapter. The industry's history is worth exploring, and you'll need to know the foundation of ETF indexing.

Along the way, we've set up some signposts to help you understand our investment philosophy: Understand risk, diversify, and know what you're doing. Our "iMyths" hopefully will dispel some common misconceptions about investing. And because we realize that learning about ETFs can be information overload, we've included "iMoney Strategies" at the end of each chapter to provide a summary and clear guidance.

Although some might argue that we have more than enough things to play with when it comes to ETFs, it's not stopping some companies from creating new tools to enliven the ETF experience. If you choose to play the market and make guesses on its direction, you can use ETFs to place those bets (see Chapters 6 through 9, 11, and 12). We don't recommend it (most people fail miserably at this), but there are often good reasons to short an index, if for no other reason than to give you some downside protection. Of course, you're not limited to profiting with ETFs when the market is doing well. They also make it possible for investors to game the swings in the market and to come out ahead even while the numbers are falling—namely, through short-selling. It's a tricky method of investing that involves borrowing securities when you believe they're going to lose value. Chapter 11, "What Lies Ahead: The Future of ETFs," is for you if you're this kind of investor. Don't worry, we'll explain it in greater detail later!

For those of you continuing on our scheduled tour, grab something to drink and relax as we regale you with a brief history of ETFs.

1

Busted: The Failure of Mutual Funds and Birth of ETFs

ETFTrends.com reader Layne Prebor is quitting his last mutual fund and has decided to take matters into his own hands: "[I] have assumed complete responsibility for my investment decisions."

One day, John Wasik had the honor of playing audiovisual geek for John C. "Jack" Bogle. John remembers ....

I had booked him to keynote a business journalist's conference (the Society of American Business Editors and Writers) in Denver, and his PowerPoint presentation didn't make it to the hotel, so he punted with some old transparencies and an overhead projector. It was Stone Age compared to today's slick presentations, but Bogle delivered it effortlessly in his dead-on, humorous style.

For those of you who don't know Jack Bogle and his amazing career, you're in for a treat. Among other things, Bogle is the Thomas Edison of the stock-index mutual fund. More than 30 years ago, Bogle had this idea that instead of guessing which stocks would do well, he would package them all in one fund: the Vanguard 500. As the chairman of the Valley Forge, Pennsylvania–based fund giant (the only one mutually owned by its customer-investors), he saw that a number of roadblocks got in the way of investors earning market-based returns.

Managers consistently made bad decisions in buying and selling stocks. They bought and sold at the wrong times. They passed their trading costs along to shareholders. Most of them couldn't beat the market averages over time. Even if they had a great year, they were probably lucky and were unlikely to do it again. This was the core of Bogle's research, and his inspired mental lightbulb led to the index fund.

So when Jack finished his incredibly precise and typically devastating critique of actively managed funds, he told John to keep his transparencies. "I felt like Moses had descended from the mountain and he handed *me* the tablets," John says. "It's been nearly half a decade since Bogle gave his presentation, but I still have his transparencies and a clear memory of what he said."

The title of Bogle's talk was "It's an Ill Wind That Blows No Good: How the Mutual Fund Scandals Will Serve Fund Owners." At the time, the acrid smell of the mutual fund late-trading scandals was a lingering stench over some major mutual fund companies (not Vanguard, though). Managers from older, established complexes such as Putnam Investments, which offered the very first mutual fund, allowed hedge fund operators to trade against their portfolios when the market closed. This was a fraud against hapless fund investors who trusted the mutual fund companies to protect and invest their money.

Bogle noted this precipitous fall from grace in his speech and added a few pointed barbs of his own. In many ways, he presaged the rise of ETFs. The trust vacuum needed to be filled. Smart investors were tired of half-truths and portfolios they couldn't see into; they'd had enough. ETFs gathered steam in the wake of the scandals and haven't looked back. Once again, Bogle laid the groundwork:

- **Cost matters!** Bogle studied the relationship between high-cost actively managed stock and index funds. The difference in returns over the 18-year period he studied (1984–2002) was remarkable. The costliest funds posted a 6.8 percent actual return—6.5 percent when you adjust for risk and a paltry 4.3 percent when you subtract taxes. In the same period, low-cost funds turned in a 10.2 percent actual return—10.3 percent risk adjusted and 8.3 percent after taxes. That last number is critical: You could nearly double your return by staying in an index fund that didn't trade. That's the foundation for index ETFs: Eliminate the management and trading costs and errors, and you boost your total return.

- **Timing and selection cream investors over time.** As if the cost argument weren't enough, Bogle found that you paid dearly for managers consistently guessing wrong on which stocks to buy and how they timed their purchases. He looked at one of the greatest periods of stock market growth and discovered that investors were getting nowhere near market returns. In fact, they were getting fleeced. In that period, stocks rose 12.2 percent. When you subtract management costs and the expenses due to bad timing (most investors guess wrong on when to buy and sell), active fund investors received a pathetic 2.6 percent return.

- **Buy high, sell low?** Most investors dive into the market near the top and sell near the bottom. Many active managers do the same. It's a strategy guaranteed to lose money. Bogle's graph showed that $1.5 trillion flowed into stock mutual funds in the first quarter of 2000, which was when the market peaked before it headed south. Was this unusual? No. The mutual fund and brokerage industry relentlessly advertised returns during the dot.com bubble, performance that was unlikely to be repeated and certainly destined to go the other way. Open-ended funds are also cursed by their organizational structure. When fundholders are selling their shares, managers must sell off positions to meet cash redemptions. That means, they, too, are forced to sell at the worst time.

Brain Freeze: We Listen to Bad Vibes

Although Bogle didn't discuss this at the time, we're hardwired to consistently do the wrong thing in investing. Our brains are programmed to be optimistic, misinterpret short-term trends as long-term realities, and see patterns where there's only random noise. We love trends. We love winning when everything seems to be coming up roses. We hate losing and have a hard time owning up to it. Denial then becomes our best friend. These components of our genome consign us to be consistent losers at investing—unless we listen to the rational voices in our brains. As investors, we can do much better. As Jason Zweig says in his book *Your Money and Your Brain,* if you've never yelled, "How could I have been such an idiot?", you're not an investor. There is almost nothing, Zweig says, that makes smart people feel as stupid as investing does.

It's possible to ignore Wall Street and the fund industry as they vie for our hearts, minds, and money every day of the year. What's important is to recognize that there's another way of thinking about investing. Instead of timing the market, forget about timing. Got your eye on a hot new search engine company? Forget about it. Most new businesses go out of business. Think passive. ETFs were born to the role, but their birth came after some rough years in the mutual fund business. Despite this investment wisdom, mutual fund companies barrage us with yesterday's returns, luring in billions when we're most vulnerable to believe the good times will last. (They never do.)

How could you have predicted when these funds would have had their hot years or their failure to repeat those stellar numbers? You couldn't. But you can see how the index investors fared. Although they didn't catch those incredibly stratospheric returns, the downside was mild—they were three times less volatile! Unfortunately, most investors would have been lured in by the returns of the 1998–1999 period, only to be burned in 2000–2001.

Table 1.1   Yesterday's Winners, Tomorrow's Losers:
Active Funds' Declines

Fund	1998–1999		2000–2001	
	Rank	**Return**	**Rank**	**Return**
Van Wagoner: Emerging Growth	1	105.52	1106	–43.54
Rydex OTC: Investor Shares	2	93.43	1103	–36.31
TCW Galileo: Aggressive Growth	3	92.78	1098	–34.00
RS Investor Shares: Emerging Growth	4	90.19	1055	–26.17
PBHG: Selected Equity	5	84.56	1078	–29.03
Average Fund Return		**76.72**		**–31.52**
S&P 500 Return		**24.75**		**–10.50**

Source: Bogle Financial Research Center

A Brief History of Mutual Fund Folly

Before we introduce our iMoney strategies, a little history is in order. No, we're not going to tell you about the Treaty of Ghent. Let's look at the history of mutual funds for a bit. Outside of your home, your most valuable assets and favorite investments are probably mutual funds and stocks. If you're like most investors, it's where you have most of your money: your 401(k), your IRA, your children's savings accounts, and your long-term savings. It's a long tradition: Mutual funds and stocks have been the investment of choice for the vast majority of Americans for decades. If you work with an investment advisor, financial planner, or brokerage company, they've directed you to them, too. Today more than $10 trillion is invested in mutual funds in the United States alone.

The last decade or so has seen a change in the air. Those warm feelings investors once had toward their mutual funds, in particular, have slowly begun to grow cold, and it shows. The trust once freely given to mutual funds has flown out the window as poor returns and white-collar crime have tarnished their reputations.

A market crash should provide lessons for every investor, although far too many have short memories. In March 2000, the stock bubble popped. By fall 2002, the S&P had declined 46 percent from its peak and the NASDAQ lost a staggering 72 percent of its gain, known as "giving back."

Mutual funds were not immune to the fall. Fund managers can do only so much to avoid having their funds follow the market. They suffered equally, to the surprise of most of their shareholders, who expected their managers to outperform the indexes. They were paying good money for the expertise of these managers, and they didn't seem to be getting it. Stock mutual funds declined *en masse,* and some of the high-profile funds gave back much more than the S&P 500. Even balanced funds, those invested in both stocks and bonds, suffered, to the dismay of investors who selected them as a more conservative investment.

Billions of dollars flowed into aggressive growth and technology funds in the late 1990s as a result of mutual fund companies spending millions advertising and pushing their high-flying funds. Remember those days when you couldn't open a newspaper or magazine without seeing a mutual fund company touting its funds? Those aggressive growth and technology-heavy funds touted glowing track records as if these exorbitant returns would continue forever.

Bubble Mania: Falling to Earth Again

The fund companies weren't dumb—they knew what they were doing during the dot.com bubble. It was a time when everyone and their brother was talking about the stock market. Fund companies were looking to grab their share of the pie, so they spent money on advertising and marketing to investors who were looking for big returns. But there was plenty of blame to go around: Investors plugged their ears and sang "Lalalala" when it came time to talk about balanced funds; they wanted to hear about funds with the biggest and quickest payoff. Because the customer is always right, the fund companies played along and gave it to them.

iMyth: Bigger Is Not Better

For years, mutual funds advertised how much money they managed. Like sheep in a flock, investors piled into name-brand, actively managed funds. People assumed that the more assets a fund scooped up, the better decisions they would make and the lower the costs would be. After all, when you're managing billions of dollars of other people's money, don't you tend to be more cautious and make maximum use of economies of scale and your huge, brilliant research staff? Actually, the opposite appears to be true. Bogle studied the relationship among fund assets, expenses, and returns from 1978 to 2002. Not only did annual fund expenses climb (from .03 percent to .80 percent over the period), but money kept flowing in, even during years of underperformance relative to the S&P 500. Even though the funds he studied couldn't beat the S&P 500 from 1994 to 1997, they pulled in about $400 million per year. These funds weren't even mediocre; that would have been matching the market average. In some years, the funds lagged the market by 10 percentage points. Bigger is not better when it comes to achieving market returns. Fund size has nothing to do with performance. Keep your expenses low and match the market with an index ETF.

Listening to chants from financial analysts that "this time is different," most of the shareholders of the hottest funds came on board in 1998–1999, just in time for the bear market's emergence from hibernation in 2000. The high-profile funds lost altitude quickly. Unfortunately, the fund companies weren't handing out parachutes to shareholders.

As the stock market decline worsened, mutual fund call center phones rang off the hook. Shareholders were holding the line, and they wanted some answers about their deteriorating savings. The mandate came down from mutual fund management: Tell the shareholders that ups and downs are natural for the stock market, and that

it's more important not to panic and to adopt a "long-term perspec-
tive." That had to be a reassuring thing to hear for someone just a few
years from retirement.

Back then, being a phone rep for a fund company must have been
like working in the complaint department at White Star Shipping in
1912, the year in which the *Titanic* sunk. The fact is, investors got
caught up in the hype of the stock market boom of the 1990s, and fund
companies did little to protect investors from what was coming. In
fact, many saw an opportunity to capitalize, and they did just that.

After the Bubble Burst: Salt in the Wounds

In early 2003, the bleeding finally stopped. But then the dust settled and reality set in. Millions of investors saw their portfolios cut in
half (or more), and they spiraled into a vortex of depression and disappointment. What followed was a psychology student's dream: a living demonstration of coping mechanisms.

Some investors just played ostrich and stuck their heads in the
sand. It was easy to play "don't ask, don't tell" and simply ignore the
statements from the fund and brokerage companies when they came
in the mail. Why not? The fund companies aren't going to call and ask
you if you opened your statements this month—especially not if things
are heading south.

Some of the most badly burned investors swore off the stock market for good. These investors considered this experience too painful,
and today they are settling for low-yielding bonds, CDs, and money
market funds, and they aren't looking back. Better safe than sorry.
Other investors just faced reality. They opened their statements, calculated their losses, and licked their wounds.

As if loading up on aggressive mutual funds and going through the
worst market decline in three decades wasn't enough for shareholders

to endure, on September 3, 2003, New York Attorney General Eliot Spitzer kicked off a massive industry-wide probe. He alleged that four prominent fund managers had allowed a hedge fund to trade in and out of mutual funds in ways that benefited the parent companies at the expense of long-term shareholders. In short, the big guys were robbing the little guys.

Bad Performance: The Final Straw

Although some of these funds have made amends and worked hard to restore their relationships with investors, trust is proving difficult to get back. Financial reporters who had been strong supporters of mutual fund investing changed their tone and started to increase their criticism of mutual funds. John was one of them.

It wasn't long before shareholders, too, began to demonstrate their displeasure with certain funds. At the time of the downturn and the scandals, there was an increase in the amount of performance analysis of mutual funds: Were they really as good as people thought? It turns out that the answer was a resounding no.

Studies revealed fewer than 10 percent of active funds outperformed their benchmarks over time. If nine out of ten mutual funds trailed the S&P 500 index over time, you might rightly ask, "Why own a mutual fund?"

Then investor advocates started measuring returns through *asset weighting*. This method looks at performance based on when you actually purchased shares. Most investors bought into funds at the height of their run-ups, then rode them on the way down. They weren't getting the returns the fund companies were advertising.

In the wake of the market decline, the scandals, and the realization that few funds outperformed their benchmarks, the number of mutual funds began to consolidate. Today there are a little more than 8,000 mutual funds, down from a high of 11,000 at the market top in

2000. Each year, 300 to 500 mutual funds are lost because poor-performing funds are being killed off or merged with other funds that have better track records.

You would have thought that the scandals chastened the industry to offer full disclosure on all their portfolios, but that didn't happen. In many cases, the directors of the funds—the stewards representing outside investors—are often the very people running the management company. That has been changing with the addition of independent directors, but plenty of conflicts are still built into the system.

To this day, you still don't know how much managers are costing investors in terms of bad trades or total transaction expenses. These are hidden from view because if they revealed the total impact of these costs, returns would diminish even more.

Once again, Bogle was right. Costs matter big-time because performance suffers. The firms that paid attention to this message have benefited the most. Ninety cents of every new dollar invested in mutual funds today is sent to one of five fund companies: Fidelity, American Funds, Vanguard, Barclays, and Dodge and Cox. None of these five companies was implicated in the mutual fund scandal. Don't get us wrong: There are many great mutual funds out there, although very few of them are actively managed. Index funds, which can be most efficiently packaged in ETFs, make the most sense for the majority of investors.

That begs the question: If actively managed mutual funds aren't meeting their benchmarks and the lack of transparency has been an increasing problem for investors, why not go straight to the source? Why not just buy the index?

Index Investing Writ Large: How ETFs Can Be Employed

ETFs got their start in the United States by tracking some of the largest stock indexes—in particular, the S&P 500, the Dow, and the NASDAQ. Since then, ETFs include everything from the smallest public companies to currencies.

Not only are ETFs sprouting up in the areas mutual funds are already covering, but they're expanding into new ones that were previously unavailable to individual investors, such as foreign currencies and commodities.

Indexes can give you diversified ownership in entire markets in one package, including products that are difficult to invest in outside of futures exchanges. At one time, only the wealthiest of investors could trade in commodities. But ETFs have made it possible for anyone to get in on the game.

Not only can ETFs give you access to investments that mutual funds can't, but they can be solid, long-term investment vehicles—if you follow our iMoney strategy. ETFs offered in 401(k) plans aren't widely available yet, although they are becoming more widely known (see Chapter 12, "iMoney ETF Portfolios"). One forward-thinking fund manager created software enabling him to manage a variety of ETFs in 401(k) plans while keeping costs low and active management to a minimum. We think it's the wave of the future.

iMoney Strategy: Our ETF Analyzer

As long as you are focused on how much risk you can take and have a good idea how to preserve your money for the future, you can ignore the stock market, actively traded mutual funds, and stockbroker and Wall Street recommendations. Pick an ETF that's broadly diversified, offers low costs, and gives you a break on taxes.

How do you gauge the best fund for you? Here are some guide-lines for evaluating different ETFs:

1. **How much does it cost?** This answer is found in the fund's *expense ratio*, a percentage of how much a fund manager deducts annually from your assets. Check the ratios of funds you're considering against a benchmark. Also, consider brokerage commissions to buy and sell shares. Here are some industry expense averages compiled by Morningstar (www.morningstar.com), a financial information company:

   - U.S. fixed-income ETFs: .29 percent

   - U.S. stock ETFs: .41 percent

   - International stock ETFs: .52 percent

2. **What's in the portfolio?** The fund manager should give you a complete list of securities, the rate of *turnover* (what percentage of the portfolio is sold off during a year), and the sectors the portfolio represents. A portfolio with 50 stocks or less will be more volatile than one with 500 issues, so keep that in mind when gauging risk. Look for sector weightings, style (growth or value), and composition (percentage of stocks, bonds, cash, and so on).

3. **What's the risk level?** Services and analysts rate risk in a number of ways. One of the most visible is standard deviation, the amount the portfolio's performance varies from the average of its peers. The higher the standard deviation, the more price variation you can expect. Several services, such as Morningstar, offer risk ratings, although it's difficult to provide for some of the newer funds. Also, look at the *beta*, which is how much the fund's return varies from a market benchmark such as the S&P 500. For bond funds, look at the *credit quality*, which rates the bonds within the portfolio. This will give you some idea how likely those securities are to default. The higher the letter ranking, the higher the quality; those rated BB or lower are called "junk" bonds, translating to higher-than-average risk. Another measure is called " duration," which measures how much bond prices will decline if interest rates increase by one percentage point.

4. **What's the risk-adjusted return?** Again, many new funds might not have much history, but you can measure risk-adjusted returns through the *alpha*. This number tells you how well a fund performed when compared to a standard for its class of funds. The higher the alpha, the better. A negative alpha tells you that maybe the fund took too much risk. Another good test is the *Sharpe Ratio*, which measures the performance against a risk-free benchmark. The higher the ratio, the better, of course, with 1.0 being excellent. The ratio tells an investor whether a portfolio's returns are due to wise investing or are a consequence of too much risk.

5. **What is the tracking error?** For a fund to fully represent the index it's intended to track, it must have a high correlation to that index. Funds that perfectly track an index have a tracking value of 100, also known as the highest *R-squared*, a statistic measuring correlation. Generally, funds with R-squareds from 85 to 100 track an index fairly well. Those below have tracking errors and should be avoided.

6. **What is the tax liability?** Few stock ETFs have any tax liability (the amount of capital gains and other taxes generated), but some do. The fund company can give you a breakdown of any taxable distributions. Keep in mind that bond, commodity, and precious metals ETFs have different tax treatments than stock funds. Of course, if you are concerned about taxable gains, you can always place your ETFs within tax-deferred accounts such as individual retirement accounts. Vehicles such as Roth IRAs and Roth 401(k)s allow you to avoid paying any taxes on withdrawals after age 59½. The catch is, you are paying taxes on the money deposited in these accounts.

The next chapter explains the mechanics of indexing and shows you how it works.

2

The Art of Indexing Using the iMoney Plan

I ended up managing some of our assets, and that got up to be a few hundred thousand dollars. I found it wasn't working for me psychologically because I was watching the Dow Jones industrial average. I like reading stuff ... keeping a finger on the pulse of things. But not from any point of view, like should we buy or should we sell?

—Ted Kennedy, ETF Trends reader

The paper came in an innocent email, John remembers of a spring day in 2004. Little did he know that he would be receiving a document from Robert Arnott outlining a better mousetrap for catching market returns. The year was 2004, and Arnott had established a reputation of being one of the best minds in finance as editor of the *Financial Analysts Journal.* He always seemed to be at the center of some debate in financial circles. With an incisive intellect and saber-like wit, Arnott would use his body of new research to launch several potent warships to attack the conventional wisdom of index investing. His discovery and subsequent application was one of the most promising developments in investing in a generation.

Everyone wants a better tool to index the market and capture the best of the winners without being stung by the losers. Arnott claimed he had found a way of doing that through fundamental indexing.

Instead of focusing on the market values of companies, he concentrated on relative value and dividends. Because he was including stocks that were more bargain priced, he told me, he could gain up to 2 percentage points more than indexes geared solely to market size.

After all, if an index reflects the stocks that most investors have already bid up, there's not that much more room for them to grow, and the downside is much steeper because they might be overvalued. It was a compelling argument, John thought at the time, but there was only one way to test it: Offer investable indexes that were based on his research. That's exactly what Arnott did, licensing his stock-picking technique and creating a whole new class of index funds. Arnott and his firm, Pasadena, California–based Research Associates, pioneered fundamental indexing with the RAFI Index Series.

In the intervening years, Arnott has been on the investment conference circuit promoting his indexes and attracting billions of dollars of funds based on his indexes. With a puckish grin, he has debated market-cap stalwarts such as Vanguard's Gus Sauter, the commodore of conventional indexing. Who has won the argument on the best index? You have, because you have two ways to sample market returns. In an interview at PIMCO Bonds, Arnott said:

> The basis for fundamental indexing came from realizing that if you weight companies by their objective size, which means your criteria are valuation-indifferent, you'll eliminate the structural bias and the return drag of capitalization-weighting. So, if you're looking for objective measures of company size that don't take account of share price or market capitalization, the list is relatively short.

For example, Arnott weighs factors such as sales, income, cash flow, revenue, dividends, and book value (the cost of an asset minus accumulated depreciation) instead of simply looking at a single factor, such as profit. Eugene Fama and Kenneth French, the creators of the Fama and French Three-Factor Model, say portfolios of small-cap and high-price-book firms are the way to go for the highest long-term returns.

Does Arnott have a better way of profiting from indexes? Only time will tell. In the meantime, let's back up a bit. By now, you certainly understand that ETFs follow indexes. But you might be wondering exactly how an index works or how much they differ from each other. All indexes are not created equal, however. There are numerous ways to look at a list of companies and evaluate how they're working together as a whole, and index creators decide who's in and who's out in different ways.

You've got the old guard, with their feet firmly planted in tradition and their "if it ain't broke, don't fix it" mentality; the new guard, who think it actually *is* broken and are looking for something different and want to mix it up a little. And then you have the in-betweeners, who are sticking by the tried-and-true methods but are feeling the seven-year itch—they want to make a change and be a little daring, but they might be feeling a bit timid.

We think it's wise to explore all of your indexing options and get educated before you officially decide what's right for you, your safety zone, and your goals. But before we get into the difference between indexes, we need to take a brief jaunt through history and explore something that's familiar to nearly every investor.

The Granddaddy Dow: A Brief History of Indexing

You have to start with the mystique of the biggest companies in the United States. And no look at blue chips is complete without an examination of the Dow Jones 30 Industrial Average.

The Dow Index, started by journalist Charles Dow in 1896, is the oldest and best-known of the indexes run by Dow Jones. Dow's creation came from a desire to create a window through which stock market outsiders could peer in. Those on Wall Street were welcome to have a look, too, but Dow wasn't so concerned with them. His index was for the average Joe.

Today there are many other indexes, but the Dow is often considered the heartbeat of the American economy. Any given day after the markets close, we can hold up our stethoscopes and listen with bated breath as the business reporters on television and in newspapers give us a number.

In some ways, the Dow doesn't look much like it did in those early days. In the beginning, it had 12 companies, but it has since grown to 30 large-cap stocks (companies with a market capitalization of at *least* $10 billion, although this can change over time) representing every major sector in the stock market. That is where it stands at the present time. At the first opening bell, the Dow rang in at a paltry 40.94. That's a far cry from the Dow of today. In fact, only one of the original—General Electric—remains in the index today.

The Dow of Yore

American Cotton Oil

American Sugar

American Tobacco

Chicago Gas

Distilling & Cattle Feeding

General Electric

Laclede Gas

National Lead

North American

Tennessee Coal & Iron

U.S. Leather

U.S. Rubber

The Dow as of December 2007

3M

Alcoa

Altria Group, Inc.

American Express Co.

American International Group, Inc.

AT&T, Inc.

Boeing Co.

Caterpillar, Inc.

Citigroup, Inc.

Coca-Cola Co.

E.I. du Pont de Nemours and Company

Exxon Mobil Corp.

General Electric Co.

General Motors Corp.

Hewlett-Packard Co.

Home Depot, Inc.

Honeywell International, Inc.

Intel Corp.

International Business Machines

Johnson & Johnson

JP Morgan & Chase & Co.

McDonald's Corp.

Merck & Co., Inc.

Microsoft Corp.

Pfizer, Inc.

The Procter & Gamble Co.

United Technologies Corp.

Verizon Communications

Wal-Mart Stores, Inc.

Walt Disney Co.

The Dow perpetuates the worst possible view of investing: that only a handful of companies represent an entire market. For the multitudes, the Dow *is* the stock market. After all, is any other indicator of stock market activity mentioned consistently during every hour of trading on radios, cellphones, billboards, and time/temperature signs at banks? Yet the Dow is neither an index (it's an average of prices of hand-picked companies) nor a good representative of the stock market.

After all, why should the most-popular signal of Wall Street sentiment follow *just* 30 companies? How could such a low number of stocks serve as a true barometer of the larger U.S. economy? Critics also argue that the Dow is a price-weighted index (an index in which higher-priced stocks have a greater percentage of impact on the index than lower-priced ones) instead of a capitalization-weighted index (an index in which the individual components are weighted according to the market price of its issued and outstanding stock, as with the S&P 500).

In a price-weighted index, for example, if a major company such as IBM has an especially good day in the markets, it could paint a rosy picture of the overall market that might not actually exist. Rose-colored glasses are nice and all, but ultimately, the truth serves investors a little better. The Dow represents companies that are popular at a point in time, not the universe of stocks.

The Dow's believers volley back: "You guys are making mountains out of molehills." They contend that, in the end, the Dow more or less falls right in line with indexes that include a bigger variety of companies and capitalization-weighted indexes. In other words: "Chill out, guys. The Dow is fine. Plus, we've got longevity and name recognition going for us. The Dow can be trusted."

Enter the S&P 500

For the Dow's critics, who remain unsatisfied with the explanations given by the true believers, one alternative exists: the Standard & Poor's 500. Introduced in 1957, it is a compendium of the 500 largest publicly owned corporations, most of which are American. The companies in this index are chosen by committee and are broadly representative of the various industries in the U.S. economy.

It's not as simple as it looks, though. The S&P 500 isn't merely a list of the 500 largest corporations. Unlike the Dow, it is a market-weighted index, and companies gain entrance based on a variety of factors: market size, liquidity (the capability to buy or sell an asset in large quantities without doing a number on the asset's price), and how well they represent their sector overall.

iMyth: The Biggest Stocks Have the Highest Returns

Throughout the history of indexed mutual funds, most of the money has been in the S&P 500, which means that investors have been geared toward an index of the 500 largest corporations in the United States. They're big, they're well known, and they're rolling in cash. Investing in them makes perfect sense, right? Not always. Small- and mid-cap stocks outperformed large caps between 1998 and 2007. Global stocks outperformed domestic stocks in recent history, by a big margin. In the long term, the differences in returns have been startling. From 1926 to 2006, small-company stocks outperformed the largest stocks, according to Ibbotson Associates. Small firms averaged almost 13 percent over that period, compared to 10.4 percent for large companies. In 36 of those years, small companies were the highest-returning asset, ranging in performance from 143 percent in 1933 (yes, 1933) to –58 percent in 1937.

Should you waste your time guessing when big or small stocks will be in favor? No, that's what index funds are designed to do in a diversified portfolio. You can own indexes represented by mutual funds or ETFs. Good reasons exist for mostly relying upon ETFs, as well as good reasons for owning index mutual funds. For the purposes of this chapter, though, when we refer to "indexed funds," we're referring to ETFs and conventional mutual funds, unless otherwise noted.

The Stock Index Universe

The S&P 500 is a good proxy for the largest stocks by market value—and has become a powerful standard for any equity money manager to beat—but it's not the most representative index of *all* stocks. There are indexes representing all asset classes, global regions, and sectors. There are other indexes under the Dow Jones Wilshire name that track massive swaths of the market, such as the DJ Wilshire 5000, which tracks more than 6,000 stocks. That's most of the companies listed on U.S. exchanges. Here are the most common index classes:

- **Indexes by market cap**—The other indexes from the S&P go well beyond just the standard 500. Do you want to obtain a portfolio of small companies with market values less than $1 billion? Then consider the SmallCap 400, the mid-cap 400, the mid-cap 600, and so on.

- **Sectors and subsectors**—More than 100 indexes cover industrial segments such as electricity, energy, health care, technology, utilities, metals, and energy. (see Chapter 5, "Slicing and Dicing: Sector ETFs," and Chapter 6, "Gold, Silver, and Oil: Commodity ETFs"). Unlike the broad market indexes, sector products enable you to slice industries down to very specialized niches. There are even ETFs for biomedical subspecialties, such as cosmetic enhancement.

- **Foreign markets**—Interested in investing in just China or all non-U.S. markets (see Chapter 4, "Overseas Exposure–Foreign ETFs")? ETFs and index mutual funds give you the world. From single countries to entire continents, you can index as much or as little as you like.

- **Commodities and currencies**—Want exposure to the incredible growth in commodities prices as the global economy gathers steam? You can find ETFs that invest in metals, minerals, farm commodities, and raw materials (see Chapter 7, "A Buck Isn't Worth a Dollar: Currency ETFs"). Fearing that the dollar will continue its descent? Indexes also track single currencies to whole baskets of non-U.S. denominations.

- **Style selection**—We're not talking high fashion. You can select a stock by whether it's oriented toward growth or whether it's a bargain relative to its peers, known as *value* (see the next chapter). So you can invest like Warren Buffett and find hundreds of companies that are considered values— but if you own an index, you'll likely own more companies than he does.

Unlike managed mutual funds, when you're dealing with an index, you have transparency. This means you can *see* what you've invested in. You know what stocks are in your portfolio. For those who got burned in the mutual fund scandals of the early 2000s, the many years of history, trust, and built-in transparency behind indexes is a welcome thing. Remember those mutual fund managers who wouldn't let you see what you were invested in more than once a quarter? By the time you saw your holdings, they were, in all likelihood, ancient history.

Not All Index Funds Are the Same

In a perfect world, all similar index funds would be sold at one low price. As you'll discover as you read on, there's a huge variety of products out there, and they don't carry the same expenses. For example, some index funds carry higher-than-average fees or even sales charges.

Do these expenses add any value to fund performance? Not at all. In fact, because generally no active management is involved in an index fund, they will only diminish returns. On a $10,000 investment earning 10 percent annually over 20 years, the average investor in a no-load (without a sales charge) index fund would pay about $2,582 in operating expenses.

Buying virtually the same fund through an adviser or broker who charges for marketing and sales would cost you $7,600 over the same period, according to the Zero Alpha Group. Why would you pay three times as much for essentially the same product? Because salespeople realize how popular index funds have become—and want to still get their cuts. Although you still need to buy ETF index funds through a broker, in most cases you are not getting gouged for additional expenses and marketing fees.

The Closet Index Peril

Another downside of conventional mutual funds is that some of the largest actively managed stock funds overcharge you on expenses while copying an index fund. How can that happen? As they get larger, big funds end up buying most—if not all—of the stocks within a particular index they are trying to beat. But there's almost no way they can outperform because they are still incurring trading costs, darting in and out of the market and forced to redeem shares during downturns.

Funds that mimic an index while practicing active management are called *closet indexers*. That means most investors don't know that they are really tracking an index and charging them three to ten times more than an index fund. The fund-rating service Morningstar has estimated that one out of seven large-company funds tracks 90 percent of the S&P 500. They looked at how closely these funds correlate with the return of the index and came up with the R-squared score. Remember, a score of 100 is a perfect match to the index, but most large-stock funds scored a 74 in the Morningstar survey.

Here's the rub: You not only pay higher expenses through an actively managed closet indexer, you also pay more in taxes because the funds generate capital gains. As a result, your performance on the active funds is up to 7 percentage points lower than with a pure S&P index fund, yet another argument for an ETF index.

What Difference Does It Make?

You might be asking yourself: Why should I care how an index is set up? An index is an index is an index, right? Just give me something to invest in. It doesn't matter one way or the other! As in the construction of a house, it matters how an index is built because actively managed mutual funds and other money managers try their best to beat the performance of a particular index. That's what fund managers get paid to do. Before fund managers even begin managing a fund, they want to understand exactly what benchmark they're trying to beat and exactly how that benchmark was constructed. It would be like agreeing to box with someone before figuring out if you're even in the same weight class. Before you jump in, it's best to know what you're jumping into.

Index Types

Traditional indexing is exactly what the name implies—they're the most commonly accepted and oldest ways of weighting an index. The most frequently talked-about index in the world, the Dow 30, has its own way of doing things.

- **Price weighted**—The Dow is the first of its kind—a price-weighted index—and it's about as traditional as it gets. It's calculated each day based on the value of all 30 companies it holds, and is then divided by an adjustment factor. When people ask how the market did at the end of the day, they're usually talking about the Dow. When the calculations are made, no regard is given to the relative size of those companies. The criticism of this type of index is that certain stocks become overvalued and others become undervalued. Critics feel that when only one aspect of a company's stock is taken into account when it's being ranked, errors will be rampant. Keep in mind that there's no perfect index.

- **Market capitalization**—The trend of using the price-weighting method of indexing slowly evolved in the 1950s into weighting by market capitalization, or "market cap." Weighting an index by this method is done by looking at a company's number of outstanding shares multiplied by their current stock price. Based on that number, the company is assigned a value within the index. The best-known and first index to employ this method was the S&P 500. Market-cap weighting tends to favor the largest companies in the United States, such as Wal-Mart, Coca-Cola, and Bank of America. It works this way: If a company's market cap is $3 million and the market cap of all the stocks that make up that index equal $300 million, then that company's stock is 1 percent of that index's value. The unofficial champion of the market-cap weighting cause is the Vanguard Group, led by its Vanguard 500 fund. John Bogle and others who believe in the market-cap system argue that weighting in this manner better reflects reality because the largest companies in the United States should be represented accurately in the index. Market-cap proponents also believe that the method gives an accurate picture of the U.S. economy and that if a stock is being over- or undervalued, it's not a big concern because the markets tend to sell at fair value over time.

- **Fundamental weighting**—As we mentioned earlier, critics of the market-cap system feel that indexes constructed using the

market-cap method don't fairly represent the smaller companies in the index because the smaller companies have fewer
outstanding shares and presumably lower prices. The flaw,
they argue, is that ultimately the larger companies will be
overvalued and the smaller companies will be undervalued,
throwing the whole system out of whack. Arnott argues that
market-cap weighted indexes are "intrinsically inefficient" and
lead to underperformance. Arnott believes that cap-weighted
indexes are only hurting themselves because some stocks
become overweighted and begin trading above their fair value,
while other smaller stocks become undervalued. Arnott isn't
alone: Several market theorists agree with this assessment and
believe it's time for a change from the market-cap system. In
contrast, Bogle believes that the markets don't necessarily
have to be efficient for a low-cost indexing strategy to work.

- **Dividend weighting**—Wharton finance professor Jeremy
Siegel advocates portfolio weighting on the basis of dividend
yields. This is another version of fundamental indexing, working on the theory that the companies with the highest dividends tend to be the best values because their stock prices are
lower relative to their peers. The risk level is also much lower.

- **Equal weighting**—One popular method of fundamental
weighting is to do away with the potential for overvalued and
undervalued stocks altogether and invest in equal-weighted
funds. In a market where small- and mid-cap stocks are heavily in favor, equal weighting is better because that kind of fund
can handily outperform the index it follows, says Timothy
Middleton of MSN's Money Central. An equal-weighted
index is an index in which each company is given the same
weight, so that small companies have as much impact on
changes as large companies.

The Old Guard Shouts Back

Fundamental indexing has proven to be a scary concept for
those who have grown comfortable with the idea of traditional indexing. Jack Bogle and Princeton finance professor Burton Malkiel, in

particular, have lashed out against Arnott's school of thought. In an op-ed piece in *The Wall Street Journal,* they pointed out a few of the problems they've seen with such indexing. Although they agree that fundamentally weighted indexes have outperformed market caps over the past six years, they say, "We need to be cautious before accepting any 'new paradigm' that implicitly suggests that the 'old paradigm'—reflected in more than $3 trillion of capitalization-weighted index investment funds—is in error."

Bogle and Malkiel believe that the notion that markets must be efficient needs to be put to rest once and for all—there have to be winners and losers. For every investor who outperforms the market, there must be another one who underperforms. In their words, beating the market, in principle, *must* be a zero-sum game. They believe that it's folly to think you somehow know more than the market, because nobody does.

Arnott says his goal is to turn decades of finance theory on its head; he doesn't buy the notion that markets are efficient and that it's just about impossible to outperform through picking stocks in the long haul. Proponents of fundamental indexing say that if a stock's price gets too big for its britches, weighting by the fundamental method won't show it, and they feel that's a plus. Fundamentally based indexes are also less apt to be affected by big bubbles or flaming crashes, which makes for low volatility and a higher return. Arnott and others argue that cap weighting "rewards companies with lofty valuations." He wants to see fundamental indexing that weighs companies by what they're doing and mirrors how the economy is evolving.

Because fundamental indexing is a way to capture unrealized stock values, it might be one of the most potent ways of reaping future returns. But like any other strategy, it demands patience and time for it to work, especially if you employ ETFs. Its virtues are simple, as stated by Benjamin Graham in *The Intelligent Investor:* "To enjoy a reasonable chance for continued better than average results, the investor must follow policies which are 1) inherently sound and promising and 2) are *not* popular on Wall Street."

Equal vs. Fundamental Weighting: The Battle Continues

Feel like you're watching a tennis match? The debate can swing both ways, depending on how you view the best way to wring profits through indexing. Arnott feels that while equal weighting funds might fix the cap-weighted problem, it can introduce a whole other set of issues: The equal-weighted funds may experience high volatility, they're capacity constrained (meaning that there is a limited number of shares, which could unnaturally inflate the price), and they result in very high turnover in some of the least liquid companies in the market. Another downside of equal-weighted funds is that when large companies are leading the charge in the market, the fund can be thrown off balance.

When a particular sector is blowing up in a huge way (think technology in the late 1990s), it could be in an investor's best interest to follow a cap-weighted index instead. What's good one day might not be all that great the next. Equal-weighted funds also have the downside of getting a little pricey because they periodically need to have their scales reset, thanks to fluctuations in stock prices. This means someone needs to charge some fees. Even so, the standard mutual funds are more expensive than both ETFs and equal-weighted mutual funds.

With experts such as Bogle and Arnott going head to head about whose method is better, where are things going? Only time will tell. Bogle feels that fundamental indexing is an attack on his legacy, but Arnott disputes that: "I see it as an evolution of his legacy." Arnott calls Bogle his hero because he "shattered paradigms and changed the [mutual fund] industry." Bogle seems to grudgingly accept the way indexing appears to be evolving and takes responsibility "for being kind of Mr. Arnott's precursor, hard as it is for me to say that."

P/E and PEG and Your ABCs

Let's drill down deeper into the fundamental school of valuing stocks. Among the many methods of evaluating where a particular stock will fit into an index via fundamental indexing is to take a gander at a company's price-to-earnings ratio (P/E), a way of evaluating a company by looking at its current share price compared to its earnings per share (EPS).

For example, if a company is trading at $83 a share, and earnings over the last 12 months were $3.95 per share, the P/E ratio for the stock would be 21 ($83/$3.95).

But what do the numbers mean? A high P/E suggests that investors are expecting higher earnings growth in the future compared to companies with a low P/E. The P/E tells you what the market is willing to pay for the company's earnings. The higher the P/E, the more the market is willing to shell out. For example, if a company has a P/E of 20, it means that an investor is willing to pay $20 for each $1 of current earnings.

Some investors read a high P/E as an *overpriced* stock. Conversely, it could mean that there's a lot of optimism surrounding a particular stock and the market has pie-in-the-sky hopes. However you interpret the numbers, it's unwise to rely on the P/E to give the beginning, middle, and end of the story because you would be left with some gaping plot holes. It is by far the most popular way of analyzing stocks, but it isn't the only way.

What's a "good" P/E? Ah, there's the rub. There's no solid answer to that question because part of the answer depends upon how much you're willing to pay for earnings. If you're willing to pay the big bucks, it means you're feeling good about the company's future prospects. But one man's high P/E is another man's low P/E. It's all in how you perceive things. It makes sense to review P/E as of fiscal year-end for several years to spot emerging trends. As the P/E grows or shrinks, you are better equipped to develop an opinion about how the market perceives the company.

It's unwise to rely on the P/E alone because many factors aside from earnings can impact a stock's value:

- **Brand**—This is the name of a product or the company. Coca-Cola is worth billions.

- **Human capital**—These are the worker bees. They add value to the company.

- **Expectations**—The stock market is all about the future.

- **Barriers to entry**—Does the company have strategies to keep competitors out or to at least limit how successful they might be?

Because those other factors come into play and the P/E doesn't take into account a company's potential, the natural progression from P/E is to the P/E to growth (or more simply, PEG). The PEG is a stock's P/E divided by its percentage growth rate. The number you wind up with expresses how expensive a stock is in relation to its earnings performance. For example, if you're analyzing a stock with a P/E of 22, and the company's earnings per share (EPS) have been growing and will continue to grow at a rate of 14 percent per year, the PEG ratio is computed to be 1.57 (22/14).

However, suppose you're looking at a stock that grew 26 percent per year for the last few years, but is expected to grow at only 13 percent for the next few. To figure out the PEG, you've got to pick a number. It's up to you: Consider the future growth rate, the historical growth rate, or some average of the two. PEG ratios are calculated by using two methods:

1. Forward-looking growth rate, which uses an annualized growth rate that often covers a period of up to five years

2. Trailing growth rate, which is gleaned by looking at the last fiscal year, the previous 12 months, or any other multiple-year historical average

No single approach is right or wrong. It's all a matter of personal preference and what information you're after. Taking a look at the forward growth rate is the most popular way to do it because investors are generally more concerned with the future.

The most important thing is to use the same method in all the stocks you evaluate so that you don't wind up comparing apples to oranges. A rule of thumb: A PEG ratio of less than 1 generally suggests a sound investment. This is all a moot point if you choose a variety of indexes to spread your bets across different techniques.

iMoney Strategy: Why Low-Cost Diversification Works

As we mentioned earlier, the big appeal of the indexed mutual and exchange traded funds is their relatively low cost, thanks to the absence of an active manager. Indexed funds are often 80 percent less expensive than actively managed mutual funds. The advantages are obvious. Indexed mutual funds aren't as high risk as other mutual funds because there's usually more diversification in their holdings. Still, as with any investment, you could find yourself in a nasty situation if the markets take a sudden spill. That means your indexes will follow close behind. In the stock market, you're subject to risk from the market, the economy, company management, and "systemic" factors, where a number of demons coalesce to cause a crash, which happened on October 19, 1987. In the bond market, you have credit, interest rate, and inflation risk. Fortunately, with index ETFs, you can eliminate management risk, the chance that a fund advisor will pick dog stocks or move in and out of the market at inopportune times. ETF providers all have their own preferences on what kind of indexing method they prefer. Some take the more conventional route: iShares, State Street, and Vanguard tend to stick to the orthodox market weightings when it comes to indexing. Others, such as Rydex, Powershares, Claymore, and ProShares, tend to create some of the more progressive indexes out there. Before making a choice, as always, it's wise to decide which method you're most comfortable with and then choose your provider accordingly. Do you want to choose a leading-edge yet unproven ETF indexing method? Then Rydex, ProShares, and Powershares could have a product for you. Looking for conservative indexers? Vanguard, State Street, and iShares have some of the oldest, most well-respected products on the market.

For most buy-and-hold investors, indexing all of the markets will give you more protection on the downside and profits on the upside.

In the next section, we show you how different index ETFs can give you this kind of protection.

3

Investing in Domestic Shares: U.S. Stock Index ETFs

I used to manage half of my portfolio, and most of it was in company stocks. When the market went down, I was holding them and I took a dive. I'm not looking to get rich. I just want to maintain the principal—with some inflation. It became clear that I didn't need to hold on to the stocks.

—Larry Connell, ETF Trends reader

John has had the privilege of interviewing four Nobel Prize winners in economics in recent years. At the end of these interviews, he always likes to pose the same question. In search of knowledge from some of the smartest financial minds on the planet, he has always hoped to discover the Holy Grail of investing, the one strategy that trumps all others in consistently beating markets. He has long stopped pretending to be a knight on a quest because the answer is always the same from the Nobelists: We invest in passive, low-cost index funds in our retirement portfolios.

The advice they give to most investors is consistent. To get market returns, you have to invest in as many securities as possible. To do that, you need a passive basket of securities. You don't have manager risk, and there's no need to guess which sector will be hot in any given year. If you need to invest in the stock market to reap growth, there

simply is no better way to do it—although, of course, there are variations on a theme. For the past 100 years, the most popular benchmarks by leaps and bounds have been the S&P 500 and the Dow. The
first two ETFs ever created in the United States in the early 1990s
were based on these indexes. Between them both, they track the
largest companies across various sectors in the United States.

Investors tend to go with what makes them comfortable, what
they know, and what they can easily check. For that reason, most of
the U.S. investments are in the biggest players, the Fortune 500 companies—all the companies whose names are most familiar to us, the
companies whose names we hear on the news or hear brought up
during business reports.

Despite global performance, investors love their homegrown
investing in a big way. To simplify things, stocks are neatly divided
into four asset classes: microcap, small-cap, mid-cap, and large-cap.

Each index provider has a different definition of the various company sizes and a different way of determining which cap category a
particular stock fits into. For example, S&P defines small-cap as companies with a market cap of $300 million to $1.5 billion. Dow Jones,
however, just looks at the largest 5,000 stocks, and numbers 751
through 2,500 are put in the small-cap category.

Big Caps: The Blue Whales of the Stock Market Ocean

It doesn't get any bigger than large-caps—companies with a market cap of more than $10 billion. They're the biggest of the big. If
Tom Cruise were a stock, he'd have been a large-cap at the height of
his career. The uncomfortable Oprah couch-jumping incident probably bumped him back down to mid-cap.

You know the large-caps: Wal-Mart, McDonald's, IBM, American Express, Pfizer. Large-caps are small- and mid-caps all grown up. The path from birth to large-cap varies from company to company. Some have gotten to where they are growing slowly but surely. Some, such as Amazon, shot to the top like a rocket. Whatever path a company is taking to get to the upper echelon, one thing is for certain: As long as the stock price continues to rise, so does the company's market cap.

The advantages and appeal of large caps are fairly obvious: Because you're investing in big-name companies, you'll get everything that comes along with the name recognition. You'll routinely see these companies covered in the financial press and on TV. Research is a cinch because information on these companies is so easy to come by.

You can also rest assured that, in many cases, you're investing in a company with a long, established track record. You don't have to worry that you'll wake up in the morning only to learn that the company has gone belly-up and you've lost every cent you invested.

The majority of large-caps are in the energy, technology, financial, and health-care sectors—a reflection of those sectors' growing importance and relevance in our economy. Baby boomers, in particular, are being catered to by the financial and health-care sectors as their generation ages.

Large-caps are generally best suited for a long-term investment because these big companies aren't growing at a rate as fast as small- and mid-caps. There isn't as much room to move when you're at the top. But in exchange for the slower but steady growth, your money buys you a measure of security.

The Middle Path: Mid-cap Companies Show Promise

Mid-cap stocks—those with a market cap between $1 billion and $8 billion—are the Jan Brady of the investing world: the awkward middle child who no one quite knows what to make of or what to do with. Although the companies that make up the large-caps in the United States are pretty much household names, mid-caps are where it starts to get a little murky. They don't have the firmly defined identity of the other caps, hovering on the brink of stock-market adulthood. Britney Spears said it best: "I'm not a girl [or a small-cap], not yet a woman [or a large-cap]."

According to Morningstar, "The best way to get a handle on the mid-cap universe is to view it as a collection of the most successful small-cap stocks and the least successful large-cap stocks."

iMyth: Big Companies Always Lead the Market

Big-caps are not consistently market leaders. The numbers show that this view is actually true: If you take a look at the Russell Mid-cap, that index's annual returns typically fall between those of the Russell 2000 Index and the S&P 500. In 2001, for example, the Russell 2000 Index had a 2.5 percent return and the S&P 500 slid 11.9 percent. The Russell Mid-cap straddled the line, with a 5.6 percent loss. They tend to be popular with individual investors because of the advantages they carry. They're not as risky as the small- and microcaps, nor are they as prone to the violent swings of the market that the small-caps are. Mid-caps aren't as big and hulking as the large-caps, either. They're just a nice, safe middle ground—the people-pleasers of the stock market. They *want* you to like them.

Mid-cap companies are typically those that have survived the tricky early stages and are on a nice, steady track to long-term growth. Bear in mind, however, that they're still medium-sized companies; therefore, they remain more volatile and less liquid than their gigant-o counterparts.

Historically, mid-caps have performed about as competitively as small-caps: Since 1981 (and up to at least 2008), mid-caps have provided 37 percent more return than small-caps, with 16 percent less volatility. An added bonus of mid-caps is greater transparency: Small and medium-sized companies tend to have financial statements that don't read like hieroglyphics on the wall of an ancient tomb. The large-cap companies' financial statements can often leave you scratching your head and wondering if there's anyone out there who specializes in translating gobbledygook.

Mid-caps have also enjoyed higher earnings per share (EPS) growth than both small- and large-cap stocks over time. From 1995 until March 2007, the companies listed in the S&P mid-cap 400 Index averaged a 12.4 percent EPS growth rate. Compare that to the larger-caps in the S&P 500 Index—they averaged an EPS growth rate of 8 percent.

Before you write off mid-caps as too "middle," consider this: Home Depot, the world's largest home improvement retailer, was once a mid-cap. Today it operates more than 2,000 stores in the United States, Canada, Mexico, and China, and enjoys a comfy perch on the Dow Jones Industrial Average. When you invest in today's mid-caps, you just might be sitting on tomorrow's large-caps. Be sure to look for ETFs with *mid-cap* in their name to be sure you're getting in on the true mid-caps.

Small-Caps: The Little Guys Grow Fast

Next in line are the small-caps, those companies with a market capitalization between $250 million and $2 billion. The majority of these stocks can be found on the NASDAQ or the Over the Counter Bulletin Board (OTCBB), at www.otcbb.com.

You face a number of pros and cons when it comes to small-caps: First of all, they have tremendous growth potential. Think about it—everyone has to start somewhere, right? Most companies don't burst onto the scene, brimming over with assets. Even Wal-Mart started as a humble mom-and-pop operation. Apple started in a garage. They had to climb their way to the top. If you can spot their potential and get in early, and if the company does well, even a small investment could pay off handsomely. Before the company gets big and institutional investors climb aboard, individual investors can have a chance to invest. When the big guys get involved is when the stock price skyrockets. Because small-caps tend to go ignored and unrecognized, they also tend to be improperly priced. This gives investors a chance to swoop in while they're still a bargain.

On the downside, small-caps can pose more risk than larger companies. You're betting on largely unknown quantities. Small-caps are susceptible to volatility, too: It's not unusual for them to fluctuate 5 percent or more in a trading day. It's enough to give an investor heartburn. Small-caps require a certain amount of research because they go largely uncovered by the media. Whereas the big companies are heavily covered, you can go days or weeks without hearing a thing about the small-cap you've invested in. However, doing your research can pay off handsomely in the long run. The Internet makes it easier these days than it used to be, that's for sure.

For small-caps, there are several options, although Wall Street and analysts still relatively ignore this segment. The available small-cap ETFs have three different approaches to investing:

1. Traditional market-cap weighted indexing

2. Fundamental weighting

3. Rules-based "quant" investing, which involves selecting stocks on quantitative metrics, sophisticated computer programs that weigh multiple factors.

The Smallest of the Small: Micro/Minis

The smallest of the caps is (take a guess!) the microcaps (generally defined as those companies with a market capitalization of $250 million or lower). They're not much like the other stocks out there, for several reasons.

The primary difference is that there just isn't a whole lot of reliable information about them. The big companies have to file reports with the SEC that are then available, free of charge, to investors. The large companies are regularly researched and written about, and you can find their stock prices in the paper. It's not the same with microcaps, and it can make them vulnerable to investment fraud schemes. Microcaps also don't have the minimum listing standards of companies that trade on the major exchanges. The companies on those exchanges need to have minimum amounts of net assets and a minimum number of shareholders.

Let's be clear on this: Microcaps are some of the riskiest investments a person can make because many microcaps tend to be new companies without a track record. They might have no assets or operations, and because they trade in low volume, any size of trade has the potential to cause the stock price to swing wildly.

A notch below the microcaps are the stocks that don't reside on any major exchange, said to be traded "over the counter" (OTC). Those stocks are dealt between individuals connected by telephone and computer networks. Unlisted stocks instead often trade on the Pink Sheets (www.pinksheets.com) or the OTCBB. But remember, we're referring to only the way these stocks trade, not the ETFs that may be holding them.

Companies listed on the Pink Sheets aren't required to meet the minimum standards or file with the SEC. They once were printed on pink paper, hence the name. The Pink Sheets generally consist of companies that are too small to be listed or that don't want to make their budgets and accounting statements public. If a company is listed here, you can bet it will be extra tough to analyze it and gain accurate information.

OTCBB stocks are like the minor league baseball teams. These stocks often have been delisted from a major exchange (usually because of financial strain or imminent bankruptcy) or are unable to meet the initial listing requirements for the NASDAQ or New York Stock Exchange. Those companies generally are using the OTCBB as a side trip before jumping into the larger exchanges.

Although the microcaps often carry some bigger risks than their larger counterparts, ETFs allow investors to get in on investing in these smaller classes without as much risk as there ordinarily would be if the same person were to invest in individual stocks. Which company will be the next Microsoft? Or the next Wal-Mart or Google? Would you rather invest in just one and cross your fingers, or invest in a fund that tracks several and increase your odds while minimizing the hit your portfolio will take if one of those companies sleeps with the fishes? We think the answer is an obvious one.

The choices for microcap ETFs are fairly limited, with just three available at the end of 2007: iShares Russell Microcap Index Fund, First Trust Dow Jones Select MicroCap Fund, and Power Shares ETF-Zacks MicroCap Fund.

Growth vs. Value: The Age-Old Question

The age-old question when it comes to investing is, "Do I go for growth, or do I go for value?" In all areas of life, people have their unwavering allegiances, and the growth vs. value stance is no different. There are devotees of both, and whatever side they're on, they aren't budging.

Standard & Poor's chief investment strategist Sam Stovall likens growth and value to the fable "The Tortoise and the Hare." The tortoise (value) wins the race, but the hare (growth) is quick and speedy. When it comes to growth, there are expectations. Just as you'd expect the hare to win the race, growth companies seem to have those "slam dunk" qualities.

Growth companies are those that are important to our economic growth, such as technology. If those companies catch on, they'll sprint right to the front of the line with a cutting-edge product or business model. The P/E is often substantially higher than average, but it's worth it when you think about where the company will be in a few years. People *love* growth. It's exciting.

Analysts apply a few criteria for distinguishing between growth and value: They take a look at the five-year EPS rate. How rapidly did the company grow? How quickly did sales grow? What was the internal growth rate? How much did the company expand? Three things land a company in the "growth" category:

- Earnings in the double digits
- High valuations of stock that investors are willing to pay
- Increased volatility

Value, on the other hand, is slow but steady. Let's face it, it's kind of a bore when compared with growth. Value is that old, reliable Honda; growth is a Ferrari. And if you had your pick of cars, why would you buy a Honda when you could have a Ferrari instead? But beware—all those extra bells and whistles can sometimes mean more potential for things to go wrong, and before you know it, you're standing by the side of the road waiting for a tow truck.

If a growth stock has a quarter in which the numbers were lower than expected, investors might get skittish and jump ship. Value stocks have a low price-to-book ratio (meaning, if you sold the company today, how much would you get for it?). Why? It could be for any number of reasons. It could be simply that the company hasn't appreciated enough and investors just aren't seeing the ongoing potential in it. But it could be that the company is having legal or financial trouble, too. The price could be low because there's a problem or because people are onto something and they want out. A company could have its stock sold off because of market panic. When it comes to value, everyone's ideal is great value at a low price. It's just up to you to find out *why* the price is so low. Sometimes it's for a good reason.

Growth is like an action flick—all thrills and big explosions. It's exciting, it's heady, and you don't know what's going to happen next. Value, on the other hand, is like a documentary: It is steadier, calmer, more collected, and more reasoned. Value, like beauty, is in the eye of the beholder. One investor's "perfect ten" is another's "Ugh! Hideous."

Say, for example, that you're a collector of autographed hockey pucks. You buy one signed by a goalie who isn't much now, but you believe he will someday be a huge star and your brilliant foresight will be rewarded with a puck worth thousands. With that puck, you're purchasing a store of value that you believe will appreciate. However, someone else could come along and deem the puck worthless, now and forever, because he believes that the goalie will never be anything more than a backup. So it goes with stocks.

Not everyone agrees where the values are, and that's what keeps things interesting. It's all part of the game. "Sometimes investors are like hyperactive first-graders playing musical chairs," says Stovall. "Sometimes they're trying to out-anticipate everyone else."

There are pure value and pure growth stocks, but even more frequently there are stocks that straddle the line between the two, known as blends. As Stovall says, "It's not one or the other. It's like men and women. Not every man is a *man's* man." Just as some men are in touch with their feminine side, and some women are more in touch with their masculine side, growth stocks can be in touch with their value side.

Leading Growth/ Fundamental Indexes	Type	Ticker	Total Assets (Millions)
PowerShares QQQ	Large-cap growth	QQQQ	$21,767
Energy Select SPDR	Large-cap value	XLE	$6,996
Financial Select Sector SPDR	Large-cap value	XLF	$5,052
iShares Russell 2000 Value	Small-cap value	IWN	$3,982
iShares Russell 2000 Growth	Small-cap growth	IWO	$3,501
iShares Russell Mid-cap Value	Mid-cap value	IWS	$3,050
PowerShares WilderHill Clean Energy	Small-cap growth	PBW	$1,732
iShares Dow Jones US Real Estate	Mid-cap value	IYR	$1,698
iShares NASDAQ Biotechnology	Mid-cap growth	IBB	$1,539
Semiconductor HOLDRs	Large-cap growth	SMH	$1,391
iShares S&P GSTI Software	Mid-cap growth	IGV	$418
KBW Regional Banking	Small-cap value	KRE	$58

°As of January 23, 2008

So what if there's high growth, but a low P/E? It's called a cyclical stock: Investors acknowledge that the company is growing, but they believe that the future growth will slow and that the P/E is far too good to be true. But it could also just be a stock that isn't very closely followed. Just as someone walking on an unexplored path could stumble upon a bag of rubies, the same thing could happen with stocks. Hey, it's not out of the realm of possibility: Stovall conducted a study showing that, on average, only 18 analysts covered every single stock in the S&P 500. Chances are good that there's a diamond in the rough, just waiting for an investor to stumble upon it, and its only crime is not being a sexy enough stock to attract much attention.

On the large-cap end of the growth/value spectrum, value stocks are typically those whose prices have dipped for any number of reasons: negative publicity, lower-than-expected earnings, product obsolescence, or legal troubles. Suddenly, investors aren't so excited about these stocks, and the numbers show it.

Small-caps that fall under the growth category are those that tend to have competitors quaking in their boots. Investors look at those companies and feel excited and hopeful. People think those companies have terrific potential to be something.

Large-cap growth stocks are the most exciting of all—just look at the technology boom of the 1990s. Growth stocks were all the rage, and everyone wanted to get in on the Next Big Thing, certain that if the Thing had something to do with the Internet, it was a given that they'd be able to retire at 25. People wanted to find the next Yahoo! or Microsoft—they wanted to get in on the ground floor and ride a company's success all the way to the top.

But all good things must come to an end, and so it did: The bubble burst and people lost trillions. And with that, a fork was stuck in the growth stocks—they were done. Disillusioned investors turned to value while they regrouped.

iMoney Strategy: Deciding on Style

Growth or value? Which works? That depends. The superior performance of value stocks is so persistent and pronounced that economists actually have a name for it: the value premium. The performance gap has yet to be adequately explained. Motley Fool's Bill Barker's article "70 Times Better Than the Next Microsoft" examines how growth and value stocks have performed historically, and his conclusion is that value, historically, has outlasted growth. The two tend to trade off, depending on the state of the economy. Growth tends to do better when things are humming along like a well-oiled machine. When things start to get shaky, wise investors will want to consider dialing it back a little so they don't wind up living in a van down by the river. Don't drive yourself crazy trying to guess which one will be in vogue this year. Index both growth and value ETFs.

In addition to U.S. stocks, you need foreign companies in your portfolio. The next chapter discusses how to diversify internationally.

4

Overseas Exposure: Foreign Stock ETFs

Investing in some areas in the world would be nearly impossible—or financial suicide—without ETFs. I recently bought the SPDR S&P Emerging Market EAS fund. I would never have invested in the potentially explosive (in both senses of the word) markets of Africa outside of a broad-based vehicle. ETFs are not only good for investors—they bring much-needed capital to the developing world.

—Scott Baker, ETF Trends reader

When Tom started his investment advisory firm Global Trends Investments in 1996, he had two major goals. The first was to identify market trends domestically and overseas, with the idea that all markets do not act in unison and do not advance and decline to the same degree. The second was to mathematically identify those trends by using the 200-day moving average, and invest only in those markets that are above their trend lines and avoid those that are below.

In the second half of the 1980s, the Japanese economy was enjoying the best times it had ever seen. From the 1970s until 1989, the Nikkei went on a bull run, peaking on December 29, 1989, at 38,915. Some savvy international fund managers held Japanese stock positions and profited from the hot bull market in Japan.

Today more than half of the global market capitalization is outside the United States. But for some reason, U.S. investors and financial advisors are still sensing that investing more than 15 percent internationally is risky. In fact, studies show that increasing global allocation can reduce portfolio risk. The major reason for global diversification is that you can reap profits from countries all over the world. The United States hasn't been the leader in economic expansion for some time, and it continues to chug along with a gross domestic product (GDP) growth rate in the low single digits as of early 2008. China has been expanding its economy at an 11 percent clip; India at 9 percent; Argentina at 8 percent; Brazil and Taiwan at 5 percent; and Australia at 4 percent. Most of the growth leaders are simply benefiting from an expanding middle class as more people move from poorer rural areas to cities. China is expected to see some 300 million people move from rural areas to coastal cities in the next decade. Other countries, such as Australia, Brazil, and Argentina, are resource rich and are feeding the Asian expansion with raw materials, such as coal and copper, and food commodities.

Where do most people prefer to invest their money? The good old U.S. of A., of course. This is despite the fact that domestic markets have, in recent history, underperformed their global counterparts. Had you been invested in global ETFs in the early and mid-2000s, you would have done well for yourself, as global economic growth continued to outpace the tepid growth we experienced in the United States.

The answer to the question of why investing in domestic ETFs is popular is a simple one: We're familiar with our country and the corporations it includes. We have easy access to information about companies doing business on our soil. Investing in U.S. corporations is easy, comfortable, and familiar. But if you want to get in on the global ETF game, you've simply got to be willing to invest not only your money, but also the time it takes to do the necessary research. You need to not only understand a particular country's economy, but also stay abreast of political developments. Are there elections coming up? Is there a great deal of turmoil in a region, or is turmoil brewing on the horizon? It's not simply about yens and euros when you're thinking about investing internationally. Because things can turn on a dime in the global market, and that information isn't always readily available, you've got to do a bit more homework than you would do otherwise diving into a domestic ETF.

Nobody is calling you lazy if you haven't gone global, because who ever liked homework? But it could pay off: Owning a few solid-performing global ETFs could help the medicine go down in the most delightful way.

It's a Small World After All

The world isn't the same size it used to be. It's actually shrinking, getting smaller by the minute. Pretty soon, it's going to look like the world in *Babe 2*, when our little porcine hero looked out his window to see that the Eiffel Tower and the Empire State Building were nearly side by side.

It is now easier than ever to get in on the globalization trend. If you want to explore your options outside the United States, you can choose an ETF to grab a piece of markets in Asia, Mexico, Latin America, Europe, or India. The ever-shrinking world and its fast-growing economies make it possible to do what savvy investors already have been: Invest globally through ETFs. In 2006, foreign, large-blend funds received close to $50 billion in net inflows and were by far the most popular offerings in 2006 and 2007.

The United States used to dominate the global economy. In 1980, U.S. companies made up about 62 percent of the global market capitalization, while international companies accounted for 38 percent. By December 2004, 50 percent were in the United States and 50 percent were outside, according to ING. The U.S. share of the global market cap is ever shrinking: In 2007, U.S. companies made up only 43 percent of the pie. As globalization increases and emerging markets continue to soar, this trend isn't likely to slow down anytime soon. It doesn't look like many people are taking advantage of the changing tides: According to a 2007 Schroders Individual Investor Survey (www.schroders.com/staticfiles/Schroders/Sites/Americas/Schroders%20Survey%20Findings.pdf), although only 38 percent of consumers think the United States will be a world leader in the next ten years, only 13 percent of Americans are currently invested in international stocks.

Emerging Markets Provide Growth

A whole world of investing can be part of your portfolio. In the model Global Equity Market Portfolio, for example, 52 percent is in the United States and 30 percent is in Europe. The rest is in Japan (11 percent), Canada (3 percent), and the category "Other" (4 percent). So we're not the only ones. There's no need to feel bad. Carl Delfeld, president of Chartwell Partners, says three primary factors contribute to the success of the emerging markets:

- **Breakthroughs in communications**—Delfeld says that when he lived in the Philippines, getting a home phone installed was expensive and time consuming: It could take up to four months to get your line up and running. For this reason, most people didn't have phones—as a result, they were cut off. Enter the Internet and cell phones, wide, gaping doors to the rest of the world. New technologies were once these countries' greatest hindrance, but they are now one of the biggest reasons for their stratospheric growth.

- **Urban growth**—In these booming countries, people are moving to the cities in ever-increasing numbers. Urbanization leads to more growth and productivity. In few places is this as evident as it is in China. As the country becomes more industrialized, its population is migrating to the cities. Beijing's population is only 1 million people off its limit of 18 million by 2020, and it's bursting at the seams as people flood the big city. Migrant populations made up for 63 percent of population growth between 1991 and 2004.

- **The rise of the middle class**—In Mexico, the poverty rate fell from 37 percent to 14 percent between 1997 and 2007. Argentinean economist Ernesto Kritz estimates that 40 percent of families in Argentina had monthly incomes considered in the middle class range, up from 20 percent in 2004. In Brazil and Mexico, the incomes of the poorest half of the population are growing faster than the average growth rate.

  The term "middle class" is defined differently in each country (the U.S. middle class is not the same as China's), but one thing remains true across the spectrum: When people enter the middle class, a cycle of growth begins. Incomes rise, people spend more, and spending leads to growth, which leads to even higher incomes, and so on. The political aspect of the middle class can't be dismissed, either—its strength and numbers are also crucial to political stability. Delfeld acknowledges that the emerging market category has seen a lot of volatility in the past, but he believes it's now in better shape than it has been in other up-down cycles. Why? Foreign exchange reserves are much higher, inflation is lower, and credit ratings and economic growth are higher. There's also less debt on the books of developing countries. For example, Brazil has paid off its Brady bonds (U.S. dollar–denominated bonds issued by emerging markets) to help reduce its debt.

Foreign ETF Expenses Are Low

International ETFs exist in a wide array of forms; all you need to do is decide which one best fits your investment strategy. For example, if you find two ETFs for emerging markets and one of them is more heavily weighted in China than what you're comfortable with, you can go with another one that spreads it around a little.

For the same reasons that many investors are still focusing heavily on domestic investments—comfort and familiarity—they aren't hip to the global economy just yet. And it's understandable. Think about how hard it is, for example, to research and get information on a domestic small-cap stock. Now think about trying to find out more about a small-cap stock in Sweden. You could have your work cut out for you.

Harkening back to Jack Bogle, it always comes back to how expenses clip returns when you're investing. It's no different with foreign index funds, which tend to be more expensive than their U.S. counterparts. A big selling point of ETFs and other passively managed funds is their low cost, and this comes into play when you get into overseas investing. An actively managed overseas fund is very expensive because it requires the manager to do major legwork to research stocks. With ETFs, after the index is put together, you can sit back and watch. According to Morningstar, the average expense ratio of actively managed international funds is 1.77 percent. The average expense ratio of an international ETF is .43 percent.

Adding More Growth to Your Portfolio

An even better reason to take a serious look at global investing is the bull run foreign markets have been on in recent years. In 2006, the Chinese market more than doubled. During the first half of 2007, the MSCI EAFE index, the largest international ETF, delivered uppercut after uppercut to the S&P 500.

"So many people are uncomfortable with emerging markets," says Delfeld. "Most people look at their portfolio as one portfolio, and because of that, everything is mixed together." He suggests investors take a different tack: Have one portfolio for growth and one for core. The core portfolio is for the safer, low-risk investments and is the larger of the two. The growth portfolio is for the high-risk stuff: currencies, health care, high-tech, and emerging markets. Having two portfolios with different objectives will ensure that if you lose your shirt, at least your entire portfolio won't go down with it.

With more than half of the world's companies located outside the United States, you simply can't afford *not* to invest globally. ETFs are making it easier than ever to get international exposure in your portfolio with minimal fees and legwork required. What are you waiting for? Opportunity isn't just knocking—it's got a battering ram aimed at the door.

The Chinese Dragon

From the early 1990s and into the early part of this century, China has been an investor's darling. The economy has been on an upward trajectory for years now, growing at a 10 to 13 percent rate between 1997 and 2007 alone. The economy has a GDP of $10 trillion, behind the European Union and the United States at only around $13 trillion apiece. Shenzhen was set up as a "special economic zone" in 1980, and since then, the population kaboomed from 300,000 to 12 million and counting. The cities resemble other cities in the developed world, with cars, laptops, cell phones, and plasma televisions available in abundance. There's no doubt about it: China is a force to be reckoned with.

The largest China ETF, the iShares Xinhua China 25 (FXI), is a large-cap blend fund tracking the index that holds the largest companies throughout China and Hong Kong. The growth is driven in large part by the population: There are 1.3 billion people, which makes it the world's most populous nation. The economy is also fueled by foreign companies looking to China for cheap labor. And the fact that China was selected to host the 2008 Summer Olympics doesn't hurt. But after the last medal is handed out, it's anyone's guess what the economy will do. Keep in mind that many analysts think China's markets are forming a huge bubble—one that might have burst as you read this.

Although no one is disputing China's stellar and rapid growth, you need to be realistic and exercise caution about the negatives. China remains a Communist country, and the government is involved in the operations of many companies, as well as the economy itself. Because of that, investing in China presents a greater political and governmental risk. The country has a long way to go before the capital begins to flow freely. China isn't cheap, either. The average expense ratio for a China ETF is .68 percent.

Some analysts predict a slowdown simply because, as China continues to grow, the cost of living will go up, and wages will go up, which, in turn, will raise the cost of doing business. It's just simple physics: What goes up must come down. The long-term economic rise can't continue forever, and it has been going on long enough that investors are starting to show signs of getting skittish. The time for the Chinese economy to take a breather could be close at hand. The country is struggling with inflation as we write this.

When it comes to Europe, you can look at it like a giant pizza. And just as it is with pizza, you have a bottomless pit of options: You can get the whole darn thing and invest in the all-Europe, all-the-time ETF. Or you can work your way through Europe slice by slice—a little Germany here, a bit of Austria there, and so on. Our stomachs are beginning to rumble just thinking about it.

Just because you've decided to go global doesn't mean you should stick your hand in every pot just because they're there. It's not like Mount Everest, a mountain that many climbers have said they climbed simply because it was there. You could lose big if that's how you approach investing.

Watch the Index

Naturally, not every country is experiencing the kind of boom that China has had. And although some countries are doing well economically, they just don't have many publicly traded companies. This means their ETFs could wind up being overweighted by the few companies that *are* on an index, and they won't necessarily perform well. The iShares MSCI Netherlands Index is a good example: ABN AMRO Holding and ING Groep make up slightly more than 32 percent of this fund. If those companies take a hit, you (and your ETF) will be feeling some pain.

Whatever countries or regions you decide to invest in, you can be sure that a lot of thought has been put into the creation of the global indexes. Market makers and exchanges providing homes for these international ETFs do a good job of managing volume and executing trades. They've done the legwork. All that's left is for you to figure out which direction you want to travel.

When you pick a foreign-stock ETF, keep in mind that some of them are subject to *tracking error*, which means they don't virtually match the index of stocks they are designed to mimic. In some cases, the difference between the ETF and the underlying index may be up to 2 percent, a huge gap in the index-fund world. To find funds that are near-matches for their respective indexes, compare the total return of the fund to the index performance. In the best possible case, the fund should trail the index only by the amount of fund-management expenses. You also see instances in which ETFs actually beat the index; some are "enhanced" for that purpose, although that's not often the case.

Leading Foreign ETFs By Assets	Ticker	Total Assets (Millions)
iShares MSCI EAFE	EFA	$51,895
Vanguard European Stock	VGK	$36,143
iShares MSCI Emerging Markets	EEM	$28,854
Vanguard Emerging Markets	VWO	$24,690
Vanguard Pacific Stock	VPL	$16,826
streetTRACKS Gold Shares	GLD	$16,826
iShares MSCI Japan	EWJ	$10,313
iShares MSCI Brazil	EWZ	$7,580
iShares FTSE/Xinhua China 25	FXI	$7,145
iShares MSCI Pacific ex-Japan	EPP	$4,105

Up-and-Comers

Emerging markets is a term usually used to describe business and market activity in industrializing or emerging regions of the world. Countries described by the phrase are usually straddling the line between "developing" and "developed." We suppose it's fair to say that if mid-caps are the Marcia Bradys of the stock market, emerging markets are the Peter Bradys: Their voices are cracking, but they're slowly but surely edging their way into full maturity.

Political scientist Ian Bremmer defines an emerging market as "a country where politics matters at least as much as the economics to the markets." Where are these emerging markets? It's an evolving list, but it includes China, India, Brazil, Eastern Europe, and parts of Africa.

The biggest and most growth oriented of the emerging markets are the BRICs: Brazil, Russia, India, and China. But don't be afraid to look beyond the big four, because there are other opportunities out there if you just look around.

At what point, though, are emerging markets considered "emerged"? As of 2006, the World Bank defined an "emerged" economy as one having a gross national income (GNI) per capita of $10,725 or more and a population greater than one million. By that definition,

China and Thailand can be considered emerged, while South Korea and Taiwan are still mired in the process. Truth be told, there isn't a clear line of demarcation that determines when a country has crossed the line into fully emerged. The whole process is ongoing. Consider China—it's the fourth-largest economy in the world, but it's undergoing a huge transformation.

Among the challenges to investing in emerging markets is that more risk is involved, naturally. Fewer shares are listed in the United States or traded as ADRs, so it's tougher to buy dollar-priced stocks. Region- and country-specific ETFs do eliminate some of this risk.

iMoney Strategy: The World Is Your Oyster If You Index

Because foreign investing requires more legwork for less information, you still need to proceed with a bit of caution. (Let's face it, though, that's a good idea no matter what you're investing in.) Be realistic about what's going to happen. When you invest internationally, you should take a long-term view of things. Make sure you haven't gone overboard with your global investments. Look at all your holdings and be sure you have a good balance. Take a look at small-caps and emerging markets, too, and avoid winding up with more exposure than you can afford based on your risk profile. Foreign large-cap funds have good long-term prospects with moderate risk. Don't forget about the tax man! Factor in your tax considerations and make the necessary adjustments.

5

Slicing and Dicing: Sector ETFs

I usually devote about three hours a week to research. Years ago, I spent a lot more time than I do now, but what I've found is that you're just spinning your wheels and making it worse.

—ETF investor Tom Lawrence

On January 23, 2007, the ETF company HealthShares had the fund world buzzing when it launched its series of narrowly focused health-related funds on the New York Stock Exchange (NYSE). Each fund consists of a combination of small-, mid-, or large-cap companies focused on a therapeutic "vertical," or a subsegment of the health-care, life-science, and biotechnology industries.

Jeff Feldman, the founder and chairman of XShares and creator of HealthShares, got the idea for the fund in 1999 while teaching a macroeconomics course. At that time, he realized that health care in this country is facing a big crisis. Through HealthShares, Feldman is investing in the innovations that might help alleviate the crisis. Agriculture, he says, is .8 percent of the economy. "Advise someone to invest in agriculture, and they'll respond, 'What commodity do you think I should get into?'" Tell someone to invest in health care, an industry that is a mind-boggling 20 times larger than agriculture, and you're liable to get some quizzical looks.

Figuring he had stumbled onto something, Feldman spent three years hanging around medical labs, schools, and conferences in an effort to learn the business. He wanted to understand the market so he would know it inside and out before creating a product to invest in it. He knew baby boomers are aging, which increases the incidence of disease and possibly even gives rise to new ones, and that the issue of health care in the United States is becoming increasingly politically important. Combine those two things, and it becomes clear: Health care, an already massive industry, is about to explode. But what part? Nobody really knows.

Feldman says that the biotechnology industry is on the verge of revolutionary innovation, especially since the human genome mapping project has begun. A number of products are in late-stage clinical trials. But trying to figure out who will be the winners and losers is a daunting task.

Picking a Winner and Scratching Your Head?

You're watching the nightly financial roundup on TV, and two analysts are going at it—again. What is it *this* time? Take your pick of arguments: Who is better, Microsoft or Google? Is eBay overpriced? Is Amazon going to continue earning profits? Oh, the squabbling! The back and forth! The statistics, the charts, the data, the analysis, the "you're wrong, I'm right." It's enough to make an investor scream that much-overused phrase uttered by Rodney King all those years ago: "Can't we all just get along?"

You have a choice, though. You can continue to listen to analysts go back and forth ad infinitum and let that guide your stock-picking strategies, as much fun as it is, or you can just acknowledge that nobody really knows where things are headed when it comes to

Company A versus Company B. There is only one certainty about what will happen: The whole thing is a mystery. No one on the outside knows if Yahoo! is secretly working on some new product that will revolutionize the Internet. Only a select few are privy to the goings-on inside eBay and Amazon.

All of this makes it so hard to choose a stock to buy. What if you buy the wrong company? What if the stock you chose gets whupped by the stock you didn't choose—the one all the analysts insisted was going to tank? Suppose there's a single industry that's poised for growth, and all you want to do is ensure that you will benefit from whichever companies emerge as dominant players?

How do you get around this problem? Sector ETFs. Instead of trying to sort out the Amazons, Googles, and Microsofts of the world, and trying to figure out who is going to emerge victorious in the end, you can play it smart, simplify your life, and invest in a technology sector ETF. Although you don't have to decide which technology stocks are going to do great with these ETFs, you've got to be at least reasonably sure that the technology sector is going to perform well in the long run. In industry jargon, sector investors "slice and dice" the market in an attempt to identify pockets of growth.

Sector investing is just one of many examples of the abandoning of old, time-consuming stock-picking strategies (following financial reports, listening to analysts, talking with friends), simply making your life easier and covering all the bases by buying into the sectors you believe are about to move into a growth period. Before ETFs came along, narrowing things by sector with mutual funds was an expensive proposition. While sector ETFs are turning up more frequently with each month, only 6 percent of traditional mutual funds represent specific sectors.

A Growing Segment

Technology is just one example of a sector ETF. They seem to be getting more specialized by the day. You can find health-care ETFs, for example—and like a boulder slowly being broken into smaller parts, cancer and dermatology ETFs have sprung from these. Then there are financial sectors, covering both regional banking and global banking. The list gets long (for a complete list of ETFs, see Resources).

Sector ETFs aren't simply for investors who have trouble making decisions: Often you make an investment in what you believe in, and your outlook on the world comes into play. If you're invested in a health-care ETF, perhaps you believe that the aging baby boom population will need increased medical care, raising the value of health-care-related stocks. Perhaps you're even part of the baby boom generation and this sector has particular meaning for you.

Or perhaps you've got a house on the market that has been sitting there for awhile, and you've come to the realization that the market has been in a big slump in your city. You're feeling pessimistic about the chances of a comeback, and it looks like the big real estate bang has gone out with a whimper. The last thing you're going to do is invest in a real estate or housing sector ETF. But your neighbor, the sunny, eternal optimist, thinks things are going to turn around any day now. He's all over that real estate or construction industry ETF—he's *sure* it's going to pay off in the long run.

You might invest in sector ETFs because of your particular views, opinions, or feelings about that sector. If you already have the larger market covered through broad-basket index ETFs, making specialized bets on smaller pieces of the market might pay off. Your odds would be enhanced if you weren't trying to pick the best moment to buy into a sector. Buy-and-holders might have the best chance of reaping returns without getting burned.

Buying Commercial Real Estate: REIT ETFs

Sector ETFs aren't just confined to stocks. You can indirectly invest in many kinds of properties through real estate investment trusts, or REITs (and you can even select REITs with equity or debt positions, or a combination of both). These vehicles own everything from shopping malls to nursing homes.... Because they pass on to investors all the income they reap from rents and mortgages, they are designed specifically as income investments. The most desirable feature of REITs, though, is not their income. REITs rarely move in lockstep with common stocks. Although they're listed as securities on major exchanges, real estate cycles rarely follow the S&P 500 because real estate is an entirely separate market, subject to its own cyclical trends. That gives you an added layer of protection for your portfolio.

Not many REIT ETFs are on the market now (26, as this goes to press), but they tend to be broad based compared to most sector funds. The iShares FTSE NAREIT Real Estate REIT, for example, represents 50 of the largest U.S. real estate trusts. That gives you geographic and asset diversification: REITs within the fund own hotels, office buildings, residential units, and public storage facilities across North America.

By sampling the real estate markets through REITs, you add another asset class to your portfolio beyond stocks and bonds. The benefits of this kind of allocation of capital are immediate because you can see the cushion of a REIT's returns during a bear market in common stocks. State Street Global Advisors DJWilshire REIT ETF (RWR), for example, returned more than 200 percent from inception (April 27, 2001) through October 31, 2007, according to Bloomberg (www.bloomberg.com). That was more than double the return of the S&P 500 during the same period.

A sector gives you a play on a number of stocks, so it's safe, right? This was part of the dangerous mantra of the late 1990s. The whole dotcom credo was, "This time, it's different." Because sectors are concentrated bets on small pools of stocks, they don't reflect the market at large, pose more volatility and, certainly, reduce your returns if you guess on the wrong sector. Jack Bogle, the father of the index fund, is one of the sharpest critics of ETFs and all their permutations. He is especially critical of the narrowly focused sector index funds, saying, "They starkly contradict each of the principal concepts underlying the original index fund …. Surely holding small segments of the market offers less diversification and commensurately more risk." Of course, some sectors, such as REITs, reduce stock and bond market risk, but you have to be careful not to load up in any one sector.

Who's Winning the Popularity Contest?

With a glance at the top sector ETFs, according to CNN Money (www.money.cnn.com), and what they represent, you can get a good idea of what's important to us and where we think we're going as an economy. So what matters to the United States and world economy right now? Here are the top five sectors by trading volume (as of late 2007) and their representative ETFs:

- **Financial Select Sector SPDR (XLF)**—XLF is the largest sector ETF. Its top five holdings are Citigroup, Bank of America, American International Group, JPMorgan Chase, and Wells Fargo.
- **Energy Select Sector SPDR (XLE)**—This ETF tracks mostly oil and gas producers, as well as refineries. XLE's top five holdings are Exxon Mobil, Chevron, ConocoPhillips, Schlumberger Ltd., and Occidental Petroleum Corp.

- **Semiconductor HLDRS Tr (SMH)**—SMH holds stock of companies involved in the semiconductor business, part of the science and technology sector. SMH's stop five holdings are Texas Instruments, Intel Corporation, Applied Materials, Analog Devices, and Linear Technology.

- **Oil Service HOLDRS Tr (OIH)**—OIH holds shares of stock issued by companies that provide drilling, well-site management, and other related products and services for the oil service industry. Its top five holdings are Transocean, Schlumberger, Baker Hughes, Halliburton Company, and GlobalSantaFe Corporation.

- **Industrial Select Sector SPDR (XLI)**—XLI follows industrial stocks that populate the S&P 500. Its top five holdings are General Electric, Boeing, United Parcel Service, United Technologies, and Tyco International.

Our priorities lay in sectors related to finance, technology, and oil by 2007, but that could change. With these and other sector ETFs, there is no need to choose between powerhouses. If you can't decide between Exxon and Chevron, why not just invest in an ETF that picks all the top players?

Not Diversified Enough to Be Single Holdings

Do sector ETFs have enough diversification with holdings of only 20 to 25 stocks? They don't and shouldn't represent your only stock position. Other experts counter that they could be useful as "fill-in-the-blank" investments. Just as even a multivitamin won't have 100 percent of every vitamin and mineral you need, no ETF will have 100 percent of everything. These narrow ETFs could be the puzzle piece you need to complete a portfolio.

The HealthShares funds are one such product. As we mentioned earlier, this family of ETFs tracks various segments of the health-care industry, including cancer, neuroscience, and respiratory/pulmonary disease. The idea, Feldman says, is to prevent disease, not just treat it. Some wonder, though, if these ETFs are too specialized.

Healthshares founder Feldman doesn't see what the hubbub is over HealthShares and criticisms that they're too specialized. "You have commodities broken down by sector. Gold is narrow. Silver is narrow. Oil is narrow. Cancer is bigger than *all* of them as a percentage of GDP [gross domestic product]." The HealthShares seek to subdivide the health-care industry in a logical way so people can invest in and benefit from things that could very well affect them down the road. Before the HealthShares came along, Feldman says, there was no future market for health-care ETFs. Now there is.

John Authers of the *Financial Times* cautions that individual investors might want to handle these specialized ETFs with care, unless they have expertise in medical research developments. They're for the investor who has the time and motivation to go over the health-care sector piece by piece. Investors should also bear in mind that, with their 0.75 percent expense ratio, these ETFs aren't as cheap as most others. And because they're so narrowly focused, they could show enough volatility to give someone a raging case of heartburn—and so far, there's no ETF for that.

Feldman says that, as a country, we *need* sector ETFs. We need narrow definitions. After all, "If everyone is buying something, who will they sell it to? There needs to be narrow sectors so people can invest and own on a long-term basis, regardless of who wants to buy it from them. You should be able to look at and customize an index."

Taking a Thin Sector Slice: The Downside

Breaking down an entire sector as finely as the HealthShares funds have is dissecting a subsector. XShares is trying to see how far it can push the boundaries. With conventional mutual funds, this would have been an even more cost-prohibitive venture than with regular old sector mutual funds. There are ETFs for cancer, cardio devices, dermatology and wound care, European drugs, neuroscience, and more, and each fund has a portfolio of 20 to 25 stocks.

Are subsector ETFs such as HealthShares too specialized? It depends on whom you talk to. Authers cites a few statistics that show there might actually be some demand for these ETFs: In its first six weeks of trading, the cancer ETF gained 18.5 percent. However, the endocrine health ETF gained only 9.7 percent in its first six weeks. Obviously, not all of these specialized ETFs can be or will be successful, but some of them could really take off, and you never know—there could be some surprises.

Our take on this is simple: Diversification is a solid idea for all investors, and we still adhere to the philosophy that you have to bet the table to win. What if you followed our advice, yet still wanted to be a little more aggressive by making bets on smaller slices of the market? You can do that and still avoid the risk trap of single companies.

The ETF industry—and the sector ETFs, in particular—has faced increasing criticism from certain media members and the old-school Wall Street-types who are concerned that sector ETFs are just a fancy shotgun locked, loaded, and aimed at the individual investor's foot. Critics are concerned that these ETFs are too thinly sliced to make much sense, and that investors will be hasty to jump on board after they've already had good runs in the market, believing that more must be better. They're worried that investors will be like kids in a candy store, running amok and grabbing whatever sounds good without pausing to think of the implications.

Bogle asserts that the typical ETF investor "has absolutely no idea what relationship his investment return will bear to the return earned by the stock market."

We take the stance that investors need to be given a bit more credit. Not everyone is going to invest in every single ETF out there, and consumers like having options. As ETFs proliferate, they only offer more tools for the individual investor to more uniquely tailor his or her portfolio to specific needs. No two investors are alike, so why should there be only, say, 50 ETFs to choose from?

iMoney Strategy: Smart Sector Investing

So you've taken a good look at your portfolio, and you've spotted a couple of holes. Or you've decided that you're not going to take sides in the various technology fights and you'll just invest in the whole darn industry. Because of their high volatility and relatively higher expense ratios, it's more important than ever for you to educate yourself about the ins and outs of sector investing so that you can get the most out of them. If you choose the sector route, this is what we suggest:

- **Don't buy yesterday's performance**—This caveat is especially relevant when it comes to sector funds because they're prone to wide swings. Sometimes they can look a lot better than they actually are. The oft-cited technology sell-off is a perfect example, but not every sector will flame out in such dramatic fashion. This only illustrates that you need to keep your expectations in check. If you invest in something expecting it to double in the next year, chances are, the only thing that's going to double is your disappointment.

- **See what's missing in your portfolio**—Sector funds are a great tool to use when you need more diversification. If your portfolio is missing something or is too heavy in another area, a sector fund could be just the thing you need to bring things back to even. Be careful, though—don't inadvertently overweight in a particular sector. For example, if your portfolio is already loaded down with technology, it's not a wise move to get a technology sector fund in there, too. It's like eating French fries, a baked potato, and hash browns in the same meal.

- **Keep sector ETFs in bite sizes**—They are meant to be more like dessert, not the main course. Don't pig out on them, no matter how tempting it might be. It is wise to allocate ETF investments as a specific percentage of your overall portfolio, based on how highly you value diversification and how you view future sector performance in the market.

- **Remember that sector ETFs are still risky**—They are subject to the same blowups that stocks are—perhaps even more so. Some ETFs can be dangerously concentrated in just a few big names. A few try to minimize the wild highs and lows by tracking indexes that use equal weighting, but these can also be limited in scope.

- **Ask whether they fit**—If you are excited about a particular sector, set your allocation and make sure it fits into your portfolio. Just because you're investing in a certain sector—say, health care—doesn't mean that your fund actually has what you want. It all depends on how the index your ETF is tracking was put together. If you're not paying attention, it won't take much to botch up your asset-allocation plan and put you in a mess.

6

Gold, Silver, and Oil: Commodity ETFs

I treat it not as a game, but it's challenging seeing where the markets are going. All these indexes you follow and you piece them together like a picture, like you're piecing a puzzle together

—Roger Hing, ETF Trends reader

John's grandmother used to fill coffee cans with silver coins.

But she didn't do it because she was a numismatic coin collector. I'm sure, being a Polish immigrant with no formal education, that she didn't know the difference between a Seated Liberty and a Morgan dollar. What was important to her was that her coins were worth something more than paper currency; their value would hold up even when Federal Reserve notes were devalued.

Having scraped her way through the Depression as a single, working mother raising three children, she had witnessed the punishing effects of deflation. Money was scarce, yet she harbored the natural distrust that most people of little means held for paper currency. The bills were flimsy and could be torn apart literally and symbolically by things beyond anyone's control. Metal coins were tangible. They had a robust weight and feel to them. You could store them easily, and they would last forever if you didn't melt them down.

My grandmother also saw her coins as an insurance policy. In a time when hundreds of stocks became worthless, banks failed, and men lived in shantytowns and rode the rails, coins held their value. When inflation was high, the underlying worth of coins tracked the metal content. In fact, if scurrilous politicians and bankers flooded the nation's money supply with paper dollars, coins would hold up nicely. I'm not sure if my grandmother had these exact observations, but she never sold her coins; she passed them down to my father, who started buying gold coins and, later, bullion, in sympathy with my grandmother's native disregard of the monetary system.

Precious metals have been good investments during times of rampant inflation. From 1973 to 1975, both large and small stocks were awful investments. Small stocks lost nearly 30 percent in 1973, according to Ibbotson Associates. Big stocks declined 26 percent in 1974, a year in which all stocks and long-term corporate bonds lost money. Inflation that year was a stifling 12 percent and then declined to single digits until 1979 and 1980, when the cost of living shot up to 13 percent and 12 percent, respectively. During those years, any kind of debt instrument, whether corporate or guaranteed government bonds, lost money to the ravages of inflation.

The gold spot price hit $711 per ounce on September 9, 1980, but wouldn't eclipse that mark again until fall 2007. In contrast, from 1926 through 1932 (with the exception of 1929), there was rampant *deflation,* which peaked in 1932, when consumer prices dropped 10 percent. The price of gold, which was tied to national currencies during that time, never hit more than $21 an ounce. Did the intrinsic value of my grandmother's coins dip then? Probably not—at least, not in her mind. That's why she held on to them.

As if led by my grandmother's unseen hand, during the inflationary spiral of the 1970s and early 1980s, I bought some gold coins and later upgraded to platinum and palladium bullion. Although I was definitely small time (no margin accounts for me), I made enough money speculating on platinum to buy my wife wedding and engagement rings. I lost money on the palladium but still have the gold coins. They don't generate any interest or dividends—stocks generated far better returns over the time I've owned them—but you never know.

Markets are full of surprises, and economies are often badly managed by human beings. Will we ever see the stagflation of the 1970s and 1980s or the deflation of the 1930s? I don't know. But one thing is certain: You need to protect your wealth if it happens again because history has this nasty habit of repeating itself. The image of those Folger's cans brimming with silver has never left me. It was one piece of economic wisdom that my grandmother left me.

Hedging Inflation: Still a Concern

Are we in inflationary times now? And if we are, how can we protect our portfolios? First of all, forget about what the government is reporting in its Consumer Price Index, which doesn't measure total housing costs and mostly ignores food and energy. How much inflation there is depends on how much *your* cost of living is rising. If your health benefits are being cut and your college tuition bills and housing expenses (mortgage payment, maintenance, property taxes) are rising, then your *personal* rate of inflation is the amount not covered by salary, bonus, or other income increases. Most households experience inflation above and beyond the government's CPI, which has been hovering around 3 percent in recent years, so you need to build some circuit breakers into your portfolio to protect against inflation. You might be able to build a hedge through commodity ETFs.

At one time, commodities were the Evel Knievel of investing: It was a fringe activity for a select few daredevils (as well as institutional investors) with iron stomachs who were more than happy living on the wild side. But it wasn't something the average mainstream investor was tempted or encouraged to get involved with. For starters, it wasn't very easy to do—commodities can be a complex machinery with many moving parts, and if you don't know what you're doing, you could lose a finger, if not your whole arm. Second, it can be prohibitively expensive. Before ETFs came along to make entry into this area easier for the average investor, commodities investing was a specialized area available only to the big players and insiders.

Demand for commodity ETFs is increasing, thanks to emerging markets, globalization, and the general excitement investors feel when there's a new vehicle. On top of the increased need and demand for oil and gas, metals demand has surged, pushing the prices of gold, silver, and copper higher. It's an attractive option; the commodities market was especially bullish in the mid-2000s. As a result, the first commodity ETF, Deutsche Bank Commodity Tracking Fund (DBC), launched in February 2006. Within four months of its introduction, it had grown in excess of $600 million in assets.

Prices for gold, silver, and copper rose quite high in recent years. There was increased demand for oil and gas. Predictably, investors want to catch the commodities wave while it's big, and financial institutions have responded by providing tools enabling people to trade in these and other commodities.

Jim Rogers, a commodities expert and trader, says that bull markets for commodities can last as long as 15 years. Rob Brown with *Investment News* predicts that demand for commodities will continue its upward trajectory for the next 20 years. If Rogers and Brown prove to be correct, commodities won't be slowing down anytime soon. Bear in mind, though, that these predictions are never a sure thing! It's always a good idea for *emptors* to *caveat* when it comes to investing. For now, though, it's a popular option with investors.

Leading Gold/Commodity ETFs by Assets	Ticker	Total Assets (Millions)
streetTRACKS Gold Shares	GLD	$16,826
iShares Silver Trust	SLV	$2,489
PowerShares DB Commodity Index Tracking Fund	DBC	$1,536
iShares COMEX Gold Trust	IAU	$1,482
Market Vectors Gold Miners	GDX	$1,437
PowerShares DB Agriculture Fund	DBA	$1,090
Van Eck Market Vectors Agribusiness ETF	MOO	$707
United States Oil Fund	USO	$486
iShares GSCI Commodity-Indexed Trust	GSG	$459

*As of January 23, 2008

The Wayback Machine: A History of Commodities

Before we talk about investing in commodities and seek to understand their attributes, it's helpful to talk about what they are, their history, and their evolution into what they are today.

By their most basic definition, *commodities* are the goods and products that we consume in some form in our daily lives. Their prices are subject to the laws of supply and demand.

Investing in commodities can be a good move for people who use a particular commodity in large quantities. For example, a giant bread factory with offices in ten states might be using up wheat like it's going out of style. They just use a *ton* of the stuff for their delicious, nutritious whole-grain loaves. So why not buy wheat futures? Yes, it's a considerable risk if the price of wheat falls, but the bread factory might just have a chance to save a small fortune if the price goes up.

Traditionally, futures contracts were designed to help farmers hedge the prices of their crops, which no one could really know in advance. Futures contracts help farmers sell their crops before they're even planted because they can lock in a future price, despite the fact that the farmer might very well get a better price in the future. From the farmer's point of view, he's hedging risk and building in certainty. When he's planting a crop that won't be ready for sale for another six months, he's wise to ensure that there will be buyers by the time it's ready for delivery. Here's where the gamble for the investor comes in: If demand skyrockets by the time the commodity is to be delivered and the prices rise, the buyer of the futures contract comes out ahead. But if everyone and their brother is growing the same crop and the market becomes oversaturated with it, prices will fall and the buyer of the futures contract could lose his shirt.

How Futures Work

Each side in a futures contract is taking a risk. Say that a coffee grower enters into a futures contract with a buyer, and they agree that on the date of delivery, the buyer will receive 1,000 pounds of coffee at the price of $5 a pound. After both sides agree, the deal is done. If the price happens to go up the next day to $6 a pound, that's tough bananas for the coffee grower (who has taken the short position in the transaction). He's out $1 a pound, and the buyer's account is credited $1,000. However, if the reverse happens and coffee prices drop to $4 a pound, the investor (the holder of the long position) is on the losing end and his account is debited $1,000. Each day, as the market moves up and down, the debits and credits are made accordingly. Unlike in the stock market, futures positions are settled each day. In the stock market, an investor doesn't realize gains or losses until the stock is sold.

Futures contracts are rarely settled with the delivery of the actual commodity, though. Most of the contracts are settled and closed in cash, and the commodity is bought or sold in the cash market.

Say that after the contract is settled, the coffee buyer still needs coffee for his own use. He will buy his coffee in the cash market at the going rate of $6 a pound, for a total cost of $6,000. Technically, the buyer's profits on the whole transaction go toward the purchase and he still pays the contract price of $5 per pound. At the contract's close, the grower can sell his coffee on the cash market and get $6 per pound, but because of his losses on the futures contract, he still really receives only $5 per pound. This is known as hedging—having the loss in the futures contract offset by the higher selling price in the cash market as a means of protecting oneself against risk.

But what happens if there are more futures contracts out there, and the holders want to settle them with the commodity, but the commodity is in short supply? Kevin Rich, CEO of Deutsche Bank Commodity Services, says that in some markets, the open interest might be larger than the underlying asset available—but most contracts are closed out before their expiration and, as a result, it's not a problem seen very often. If the seller of a contract was unable to deliver a physical commodity, the issue would be dealt with by the compliance department of the exchange where the contract was listed and with the physical delivery point where the settlement was supposed to take place.

Down on the Farm: Food-Based Commodities

Modern commodity trading has its roots in agriculture: Wheat, corn, pigs, and cattle were traded extensively in the 1800s. The whole concept of dealing in commodities is believed to date back to ancient Sumerian times, when people traded clay tokens in the shape of sheep or goats. A certain number of tokens was placed in containers, and the tokens became a sort of "I.O.U.," a promise to deliver the commodity equal to the number of tokens held in the container. The delivery was to be made on a certain agreed-upon time and date, which is a similar concept to the futures contracts we all know and love today.

In North America, the futures market evolved into what it is today out of sheer necessity. Before futures, farmers grew their crops and brought them to market, crossing their fingers that there would be enough buyers. Trying to gauge the demand for a given crop was a guessing game, and the farmers often found that they had too much— the unpurchased crops, being perishable, were lost for good. At other times, farmers found masses clamoring for a given crop and they didn't have enough to go around, which drove up the prices.

Someone finally said, "This is nuts—we have to do something!" That's when the forward contract was born. The forward contract eventually evolved into the futures contract, but it worked in much the same way: It was a concept created to help protect farmers against a loss by enabling them to accurately gauge supply and demand, thus giving crop prices a measure of stability.

The oldest official futures exchange in the world is the Chicago Board of Trade, which was founded in 1848 with contracts covering flour, timothy seed, and hay. The Chicago Mercantile Exchange was born in 1898 as the Chicago Butter and Egg Board. Care to hazard a guess as to what it traded?

Commodities today have evolved from being limited to those crops and other perishable basics, and the market has extended well beyond the local marketplace of the 19th century. It isn't just farmers playing the game anymore. Today, thanks to technology and the Internet, commodities are a worldwide venture, involving importers, exporters, manufacturers, speculators, and more. It's as much for the people creating a particular commodity as it is for the people who use it and the speculators or hedgers who seek to profit from their fluctuations in price.

iMyth: You Can Predict Commodities Prices

At this point, you must be wondering how to tell which commodity you should be invested in at any given time. There's the rub— as with most other areas of investing, you just never really know what's going to happen. John Schoen of MSNBC cites the example of summer 2007 gas prices, when it seemed as though they were playing a rousing game of limbo. Many invested in gasoline futures—and lost money. They were snookered by news reports in the months leading up to that summer about how gas prices would rise dramatically. After all, the price of gas going up in the summer is about as traditional as a barbecue on the Fourth of July. A CNN Money article that ran on April 26, 2007 quoted industry experts predicting that the price of gas could hit $4 a gallon in some locations. It wasn't just idle speculation, of course. According to another CNN Money article, a new refinery hasn't been built in the United States since 1976. Since then, demand for gas has gone through the roof. In 2005, American drivers burned 36 million more gallons of gas than the country produced. The difference is covered by imports. In short, the multimillion-gallon difference and the heightened summer demand, coupled with a lack of space to keep up with that demand, pushes up the prices each year. So what happened? Much of the speculation was based on past history. In 2005, Hurricane Katrina drove gas prices to new, stomach-churning highs. In July 2006, an Israeli invasion of Lebanon caused crude oil prices to hit $76 a barrel, meaning gas prices weren't far behind. This example illustrates all the factors that come into play when it comes to commodities and the sudden, unforeseen political events and natural disasters that can cause the market to turn on a dime. So many things influence commodity prices that you can't track them all. Leave that to the professionals.

Knowing the Risks

You know you can get in way over your head when the people who deal in commodities as a way of life struggle to pinpoint the movements of the market and make predictions about the future. That's why it's important to understand how the machine works before you begin using it, if you decide you still want to proceed.

Commodities can be an especially volatile trade, even in the most bullish of times. All it takes is one major weather event or a major shift in the global economy to have a huge impact on a given commodity. If you can handle the stomach-churning roller-coaster ride, though, it can be exhilarating.

As another alternative of sector trading, commodities have a life and a lexicon all their own. They are an industry with high volatility, and it certainly hasn't been for the faint of heart or the inexperienced trader. Although you have the opportunity to do fantastically well in these products, you have an equal opportunity to take hits big enough to reduce a grown man to wracking sobs. And if you can't take the hog futures, stay off the farm. Or something like that.

How Commodity ETFs Work

Thanks to commodity ETFs, you have been granted an all-access pass. If you wanted to play the game before, the most common way to go about doing so was through the buying and selling of individual futures contracts which are very expensive, complicated, and volatile. You would put a portion of cash on margin against the total value of a contract, based on its future value (as opposed to its current value).

If the price of the commodity went up, you were sitting pretty. If it went down, however, you would need to dig deeper into your pockets to cover the difference. And if you didn't roll over your contract (which means trading in your old contract for a new one before the date of delivery), you could conceivably wind up with the commodity you invested in right at your doorstep. Pigs are cute and all, but where would you store them? It's a key difference between investing in stocks and trading in commodities. If you own stock in a company, you can hold it for as long as you please and do nothing with it until the end of time.

Beginning in February 2006, ETFs allowed individual investors to get into commodities investing with the creation of the first commodity-linked index fund. The PowerShares DB Commodity Index Tracking Fund (DBC) uses futures contracts to mirror the Deutsche Bank Liquid Commodity Index, which was originally made up of 35 percent crude oil, 20 percent heating oil, 12.5 percent aluminum, 10 percent gold, and 11.25 percent each on corn and wheat (subject to periodic adjustments).

Before you start buying, though, understand that commodities ETFs are a completely different animal than futures contracts. For one thing, they don't follow an index made up of companies. They follow a basket of commodities (as in the case of the DBC fund mentioned earlier). ETFs that use futures contracts have uninvested cash, which is usually placed in interest-bearing government bonds. That interest is used to cover the expenses of the ETF and to pay income to the shareholders. You can also invest in the producers of a certain commodity, such as gold-mining companies.

But why explore commodity ETFs? Kevin Rich, CEO of DB Commodity Services, explains, "Most investors looking at asset allocation want to create a diversified portfolio." Aside from the diversification a commodity ETF offers, it eliminates or minimizes much of the cumbersome aspects of commodity trading.

"Everything that's true of regular ETFs is also true of commodities ETFs," says Rich. "They're low cost and transparent."

You can own commodities such as gold by buying bars and storing them, but that isn't practical with perishable commodities such as agricultural products or those that are otherwise difficult to store. (Cows, anyone?) Buying a commodity ETF that tracks a futures index makes the process easier and keeps the space in your home free for other things. The manager of that ETF has to do the heavy lifting: looking at prices, rolling over contracts, and generally making sure investors are getting a return on the money they've put in. It's like letting a NASCAR racer drive his car in circles instead of hopping behind the wheel to do it yourself. It's not as exciting, but don't you feel safer watching the race from the comfort of the grandstand?

Commodity ETFs require more management than traditional ETFs, but Rich says you can't compare the two otherwise. "It's a very active process, with many moving parts. When you compare the expenses of commodity ETFs, you need to compare them to commodity trades. It's not always apples to apples."

Rich says what really needs to be compared are the expenses of commodity ETFs versus direct commodity trades. "Competition has led to a reduction in costs. It was hard to get in for less than 2 percent (annual expense ratios) before, but now the majority can get in for less than 1 percent per annum. It has become even more cost effective."

Tax Treatment Different for Commodity ETFs

Because they're not tracking indexes composed of stocks, commodity ETFs might translate into higher tax rates. They're tracking futures, and 40 percent of the gains on futures contracts are taxed at short-term capital gains rates. Gold and silver ETFs are taxed not as securities, but as collectibles, meaning that long-term capital gains on those funds are taxed at a maximum rate of 28 percent instead of the lower 15 percent rate for stocks. As if that weren't enough, instead of being set up as registered investment corporations like most stocks at ETFs are, U.S. Oil is set up as a partnership and iShares funds are organized as limited liability companies. Under those setups, shareholders have to pay taxes each year on the gains and income the funds earn—even if they aren't distributed. In short, you could be paying taxes on money you didn't even get.

The Golden Ticket: Precious Metals ETFs

Gold has long been one of the most popular commodities investments around, and the reasons for its popularity have remained unchanged through history: Gold is an excellent hedge when the economy is shaky. When it's included in your portfolio, it lowers your overall risk because it's a good hedge against inflation over the long term.

In gold ETFs, the fund doesn't have to trade actual, physical gold. Before the advent of the gold ETF, gold was physically bought and sold in bullion. If you invested in gold, you owned gold you could hold in your hands. That's fun for about five minutes, but then it becomes a little cumbersome. The launch of the streetTRACKS Gold Shares (GLD) in 2004 was met with plenty of controversy. Some people were excited at the prospect of gold being opened to greater investor participation. Others thought it was a ploy to suppress gold by steering capital away from the physical commodity and into a piece of paper.

Here's where commodities ETFs get a little weird and confusing. Regular ETFs are designed to track the price of their underlying assets—generally, an index. But in the case of commodity ETFs, the underlying asset has its own supply and demand that is completely separate from the ETF's supply and demand. For example, more people might want actual oil than people who want to own an ETF that tracks the price of oil. When you know this, you won't find it as surprising that, in the GLD's first year of existence, it didn't follow the five separate dips gold itself took. In other words, a commodity index may not track the price of the underlying product closely. That's called "tracking error," which is more of a problem outside of stock and bond indexes.

Many types of inflation can ravage your nest egg. Rising wages, higher energy prices, and rising interest rates are all examples. Commodity ETFs can hedge against the increase in the prices of materials and general inflation. One simple relationship is found between rising gold prices in times when expectations of U.S. inflation escalate, causing the value of the dollar to drop. Crude oil prices have topped $100 a barrel; the dollar hit all-time lows against the euro and yen in 2007. Nearly every major industrial commodity hit record highs as well that year, due to ever-higher demand in developing countries. And gold has climbed back to its early 1980s levels, hitting $850 an ounce. Commodity ETFs protect your purchasing power and create profits from these developments. But you have to be especially careful with them. Don't try to bet on price swings and hold them long-term as a hedge against inflation.

7

A Buck Isn't Worth a Dollar: Currency ETFs

I handle my wife's investing. I've been messing with this kind of thing since 1978. I use a spreadsheet, keep track, run the market. I track about 85 ETFs and several mutual funds. I am 100 percent international. Nothing domestic.

—Bob Grayson, ETF Trends reader

Because of its huge national debt, trade surplus, and the government's constant need to borrow money, the greenback was no longer on the top of the heap by late 2007, in terms of currency values. Ever since the dollar was delinked from gold reserves in the 1970s, its value has been floating in a sea of other currencies.

As a reserve currency—that is, one that is used as a denomination for things such as world oil prices and government surpluses—the dollar has been considered a reliable international economic bulwark. That's becoming less the case as the subprime mortgage crisis and congressional inability to trim deficit spending continue to tell investors around the world that the American government, industry, and consumers can't get a handle on their debt addiction. For nearly a decade, Congress and the White House have borrowed to finance personal tax cuts, the Social Security/Medicare trust fund, and wars in

Iraq and Afghanistan. Even imported oil is paid for by borrowed money. Who's paying for government spending? Mostly the Chinese government and other foreign investors, which have bought about $1 trillion in U.S. debt.

Like all debt dilemmas, the tide will turn and either the dollar will strengthen or foreign holders of Treasury securities will start dumping them on the market. By the end of 2007, OPEC, the cartel of oil-producing nations, was discussing denominating crude oil prices in a currency other than the dollar because the buck's decline was partially responsible for boosting the crude price above $90 per barrel that year.

The U.S. dollar has taken a couple of roundhouse kicks to the fore-head in recent years. That has hastened the development of currency ETFs. At the end of 2005, Rydex launched the first currency ETF, the Euro Currency Trust. Since then, currency ETFs have been formed to track the Swedish krona, Australian dollar, Mexican peso, and Canadian dollar, to name just a few. Although it's tempting, investors shouldn't just dive into the most high-profile currency ETF—the euro, as of 2007. While the euro's skyrocketing value was enjoying good press, it was also being outperformed by several other currency ETFs. It's just a reminder to do your research and look before you leap, and to always remember that the currency market is very fluid. Things aren't always as they appear to be. And stay tuned—there are more currency ETFs to come.

Instead of just staying flat, the world's currencies are always shifting in value, independently of one another, rising one day and falling the next. If the dollar becomes worth a little more one day, it has no bearing on whether the yen falls or rises that same day. Investors can exploit these differences in values, which is one of the prime reasons for currency ETFs.

A Brief History of Currency ETFs

Currency investing is yet another area that was mostly closed off to the individual investor before ETFs were introduced. The foreign exchange, or FOREX, used to be for the big players, such as banks. Investing in currency before ETFs was an expensive logistical challenge, more than what an individual investor might have been able to handle or willing to tackle. But now that the individual investors have been given access to a buffet of currencies, they're giddy, and currency ETFs have taken off like gangbusters. That's not necessarily a good thing, though.

Rydex introduced the first currency ETF in December 2005. By November 2006, there were seven ETFs tracking underlying currencies and they had reached the $1 billion milestone. It's safe to say that investors were hungry—no, *starving*—for a chance to invest in currencies because, by December 2006, there were 15 currency ETFs, with more on the way. If the dollar's value becomes weaker against some foreign currencies, these ETFs will only grow in popularity as investors seek to capitalize on the trend with previously unseen ease. (*Disclosure:* Tom is a member of the Rydex board of directors.)

Back to Basics

Let's pretend you're holding a dollar bill in your hand. That note represents a store of value, and it's no different anywhere else in the world. Money stands for something; it means something. Whoever said "Money talks" wasn't kidding.

Each country or region has a currency zone, which is an area where a specific currency is the dominant means of exchange. Japan has the yen, Great Britain has the pound, Sweden has the krona ... you get the idea. Because each currency around the world has a different value, you can exchange one currency for a different currency at the current exchange rate, which fluctuates daily. (To find current exchange rates between currencies, go to www.x-rates.com.) This is why, if you pay a visit to a country where the currency is worth more than the dollar—let's say it's England—you'll pay a pretty penny for that plate of fish 'n' chips. (The dollar was worth half as much as the pound by the end of 2007.) But likewise, our dollar being cheap isn't all bad: It can help boost tourism here. Those tourists may very well spend more than they would ordinarily as they find themselves flush with our cash.

Most countries maintain control over their own currency. The largest exception to the rule is the European Union's Economic and Monetary Union. It has ceded control of the euro to the European Central Bank (www.ecb.int). In the United States, the monetary authority is the Federal Reserve System (www.federalreserve.gov). In theory, monetary authorities operate without direct interference from the legislative or executive branches. However, the monetary authority was brought into the world by the government, and it can be taken right back out, as unlikely as that might be. In the Western world, the monetary authority is more or less independent.

Countries can and do use the same name for their currency. (For example, Canada, Australia, and the United States call their currency the dollar.) Groups of countries can use the same currency (the euro is the perfect example), and a country can declare the currency of another country to be legal tender. (For example, Panama uses the U.S. dollar as its official currency.)

Making It Personal

Currencies move independently of one another, so you might be wondering why it all really matters. In the early part of this century, the U.S. dollar has been weak relative to other currencies, and the

British pound has been worth more. Not many Americans will find themselves on the other side of the pond on vacation. When it costs $2 to convert to a single British pound, it's bound to put a bit of a crimp in your travel plans. However, because our dollar is so cheap these days, we could expect an influx of British tourists who are more than happy to spend their hard-earned money on our goods and services. As you can see, even if the dollar is beaten down a bit, it isn't *all* bad.

There are other implications, though. Imports and exports can suffer when two currencies have vastly different values. With a weak dollar, Americans may be less inclined to purchase Louis Vuitton bags, BMWs, and other luxury goods manufactured in countries with much stronger currencies. Americans become nervous that the same dollar that could have purchased a Louis Vuitton luggage set can now net only a small wallet, and they begin to search for a better deal. Meanwhile, manufacturers in other countries with stronger currencies become nervous because their U.S. sales are down.

iMyth: Foreign Currencies Don't Impact Your Life

When the dollar is strong, consumers will see lower prices on foreign products and services, but U.S. companies will find tougher competition in foreign markets. When the dollar is weak, it's easier for the United States to sell its wares in other countries. U.S. companies may not be able to expand in foreign markets. It doesn't make sense to root for the dollar's value to be one way or the other. Consistently predicting which way currencies will go is a bit like forecasting commodities or stock prices. No human being has come up with a foolproof method of charting the future on a day-to-day basis. And those who think they know how to do it are usually wrong. The bottom line is that when a currency loses value relative to other currencies, it's inflationary. That means the cost of living rises in an unseen way.

How Currencies Are Valued

Who, exactly, determines the values of these currencies? Is there someone who wakes up each morning and decides, "I think the U.S. dollar shall be worth four times the euro today"? It would be nice for us, but, no, that isn't how it works. Currency values are determined by a number of wide-ranging factors:

- **Political conditions**—How stable is the government? Is it corrupt? Can it be bribed? Does the country play well with others, especially the big players, such as the United States, China, and Russia? Take a look at the form of government: Is it a dictatorship? Communist? A democracy?

- **The economy**—The unemployment rate, the country's overall work ethic, inflation, and the general direction of the economy are factors. Also, is the country older or newer? What is its chief industry (technology, agriculture, manufacturing)? Does its government run a budget/trade surplus or deficit? Does it have to borrow heavily? Are interest rates going up or down within the monetary system (up is bullish for the currency)?

- **Outside perception**—Appearances shouldn't matter, but, like it or not, they do. Perception might have no basis in reality, but things like news reports, movies, newspapers, and good old-fashioned rumors can affect how a country appears to the rest of the world. Another factor in a currency's value is how much is known about its country. The less is known, the lower the value. This is one instance when it doesn't pay to be an enigma.

- **Demographics**—A young population tends to signal a bright future full of people who are open to growth, new ideas, and change.

- **Public figures**—Whether leading the country or just merely famous, the best-known people in a country can hold great sway over how their homeland is perceived.

- **Level of openness**—Privacy costs a country currency. Cuba is isolated and has been for some time. China is becoming more open. Venezuela is becoming more isolated. If a country is slowly becoming closed off from the outside world, its currency will suffer.

- **Natural resources**—How in demand is a country's resources? If value is perceived (whether legitimately or not), the currency will go up.

- **Weather**—Not only is the type of weather and its severity important, but how a country responds to weather-related disasters is a factor in its currency value. This affects how the outside world perceives them, and the country be a less-attractive tourist destination if its response to disaster is poor.

- **War and conflicts**—Who are the country's allies? Who are its enemies? How strong is the military? Is it at war or experiencing civil conflict, border disputes, internal genocide, and other problems?

- **Education**—The level of education of a country's population affects the value of the currency. How connected are the people to the Internet? Do they speak a number of languages? Does the country have a lot of scientists, inventors, and authors?

Turn Dollars into Lemonade

Remember that global boom we were talking about earlier? How emerging markets are on the rise and the economies of other countries are slowly outpacing the U.S. economy? Investing domestically these days doesn't make much sense when countries such as China are leading the charge in key areas such as manufacturing growth and natural resource development. Now is the time to take advantage of the gradual but sure-footed shift to a global economy and to begin investing in currency ETFs. As with the ETFs that follow an index, currency ETFs allow investors to take advantage of the "If you can't beat 'em, join 'em" approach. That is, take the dollar's lemons and turn them into lemonade.

Currency ETFs have grown especially popular in the time since the first such fund was launched because, aside from the diversification they offer, investors enjoy taking advantage of international interest rate adjustments and geopolitical issues. Assets are pouring into currency ETFs because investors are realizing the risk of investing in only one currency. That's nothing but a game of Russian roulette.

Currency ETFs aren't created willy-nilly; a certain amount of thought and research goes into them. Tim Meyer, ETF business manager at Rydex, says that when analysts are looking at which currency ETFs to offer, "We look at what's most liquid. The reason is that the less liquid [they are], the less opportunity there is to offer something as an ETF."

Stephen Sachs, Rydex's director of trading, said the main advantage to trading with a currency ETF is the same advantage offered to other ETFs: transparency. The exchange is listed and everyone gets the same price, unlike when you attempt to buy currency in a foreign country and get a little bit ripped off. Since there's only a minimum shade of one share, the investment one must make is much smaller than in a typical foreign exchange trade.

iMoney Strategy: Betting Against the Dollar

It's all speculation, of course, that the dollar will continue its decline against other currencies around the world. But if you're feeling certain that it will, you can invest in a currency ETF and essentially bet that the foreign currency will rise and that the dollar will weaken against it. Worldwide currency can be volatile and can be affected by a wide range of factors, but currency ETFs can give you a way to bet against the U.S. dollar and gain foreign market exposure without betting and possibly losing the entire farm. If you feel that you're ready to get involved, here's what you should know:

- Currency ETFs have different tax rules than regular ETFs. Interest income as well as gains are taxed at the ordinary income tax rate rather than at the long-term capital gains rate.

- Read the newspaper—and not just the financial section, You need to study and know the political situation of the country's currency you've invested in. Some areas are more volatile than others, but you should always pay attention to the factors that could determine whether the currency rises or falls.

- Don't put all your eggs in one basket. Chuck Butler, president of EverBank World Markets, recommends that his clients don't have more than 20 percent of their net worth in a foreign currency. We recommend one fund that indexes several currencies.

- Hang on! Patience is a virtue. Don't dive in and out of ETFs hoping to score big. Buy and hold. Know how much risk is involved.

- Keep in mind that many IRA-qualified accounts don't typically permit currency trading, and institutions are often restricted from holding certain assets, but they *are* permitted to hold ETFs. *Voilà* the currency ETF solves that problem, and everyone wins while still following the rules.

8

Getting Chunks of the Bond Market: Fixed-Income ETFs

ETFs are effective in targeting the market that you want to invest in because they cover such a broad range and a narrow scope. You can ... pick something single, like gold; you can pick a country; you can pick broad or narrow areas of investing in a very efficient and cost-effective way.

—Peter Tolk, ETF Trends reader

You might be familiar with savings bonds, those checks you'd get every year on your birthday and possibly even at Christmas. Grandparents loved them. Tom's grandparents would consistently tell him, "You can have this [the bond] when you're 18, and it's worth what it says on the front!" And he'd think, "Gee, *thanks.*" When you're 7 years old, 18 is just about the last age you reach before death. But then you go to college, and you realize all those savings bonds are going to pay for your $250 organic chemistry textbook, and suddenly you're thanking your grandparents for their foresight without the least bit of sarcasm.

What happened between the year you grudgingly received the savings bond and the year you cashed it? Your grandparents bought those savings bonds for half their face value (for example, a $50 bond costs $25), essentially loaning the government money. The money earns interest over a period of years, and when the bond is mature, or worth its full face value, you cash it out and enjoy the money. We suggest treating your grandparents to a nice lobster dinner in the unlikely event that there's anything left over after textbooks.

This is pretty much what bonds are: a form of borrowing with an obligation behind them. Someone is borrowing money from a person or entity and then paying it back over a specified period of time at a specified interest rate. Savings bonds aren't the only ones out there. Certificates of deposit aren't bonds but are similar to them. Treasury bonds are backed by the federal government. Municipal bonds are offered by municipalities—school districts, utilities, states, counties, localities, and so on. Corporate bonds are often used by companies to raise money for research and development, or to fund expansion when profits are not enough, and these are backed by the corporation's equity; debentures are unsecured corporate bonds. Money market funds are made up of a variety of government, corporate, and banking "paper"—short-term bonds, certificates of deposit, bankers' acceptances, repo agreements, and so on.

Slow to Take Off

Many stock investors don't quite seem to understand bonds, and vice versa. Stocks and bonds are completely different things; they're treated differently and they're not attractive to the same types of investors.

Until 2007, the market for fixed-income ETFs was fairly limited. Investors were mostly interested in tracking the standard indexes before tackling the new and innovative types of ETFs that track commodities, currency, and now bonds. iShares was the first choice for investors seeking to invest in the bond market via ETFs. The provider later expanded the number of funds it offers, and the fixed-income ETF universe more than doubled. Their competitors have caught on, and other ETF providers are frequently adding new funds to the pipeline. Fixed-income ETFs are just another example of how ETF providers are actively seeking new ways to explore just what ETFs are able to do.

Barclays iShares offers the largest number of bond ETFs, which offer good coverage and credit quality for most investors. State Street Global Advisors began to offer the Lehman International Treasury Bond ETF in October 2007.

What's true for ETFs in general also holds true for bond ETFs: They still have a low trading cost and exchange traded prices. They give investors the ability to diversify their portfolios.

According to David Levine, author of *The Radical Guide to Bonds*, you must consider three points with indexed bond ETFs:

- **Costs are generally low.** Expense ratios for bond ETFs are .15 to .20 percent, depending on a few factors such as credits and maturities in the bond index. But the more specialized a bond ETF becomes, the higher the expense ratio goes, simply because the fancier you get, the more upkeep is required.
- **Distributions should be primarily interest income.** In looking at the distribution history of Barclays broad-based indexed bond ETF, no short- or long-term capital gains have been distributed; only interest has come back. But don't get excited: This doesn't mean that no capital gains will be distributed in the future. It will still hold true, however, that the meaningful distributions on indexed bond ETFs will be interest, not capital gains.
- **Additional trading costs could be passed on to you.** Just as with mutual funds, the annual ETF expense ratio doesn't include trading costs the managers rack up. And they aren't doing it for free.

Why Bonds?

Bonds are for long-term investors, the ones who are thinking 10, 20, and however many years into the future. They're thinking about their children's college education. They're thinking about their own retirement and want to ensure that they've still got money coming in long after the last slice of cake has been dished out on their last day of work. They're thinking about debt and mortgages that they might still need to pay off. Individual investors looking at bonds are looking at a security blanket for the expenses of the future, the ones they know about and can plan for so they're prepared when a kid says she's going to Harvard, but not on scholarship. Ouch!

The majority of bond investors are in it for the long haul. If you've got similar issues coming up (you *do* want to retire, don't you?), you might consider adding bond investments to your portfolio as well. They're considered a fairly safe and, if done well, low-cost way to invest in your own peace of mind.

In mutual funds and ETFs made up of bonds, there are varying yields and rates of maturity. ETFs make it possible to invest in bonds while staying diversified with lower risk. They're like the big balance bar trapeze artists use to walk the tightrope: Bond ETFs keep an investor's portfolio steady instead of crashing into the net below. And because the ETF package trades on the exchange like a stock, you don't have to be locked in for the duration of a long-term bond.

Municipal Bonds

Municipal bonds, also known as munis, are a lure for many investors because the interest income is exempt from federal income tax and, if the bonds are from municipalities within the state where you live, also exempt from state and local taxes. They're even more appealing when the interest and principal payments are guaranteed by AAA-rated municipal bond insurers. Thanks to their tax status, municipal bonds are of interest to investors in the higher tax brackets. According to a study by the SEC, the five largest state issuers of municipal bonds are also the five states with the largest populations over age 65 (California, New York, Texas, Florida, and Pennsylvania). Because they contain the tax-free feature, yield on munis will be lower than for other types of bonds. Be sure to perform an after-tax comparison to decide whether the tax-free or taxable yield comes out better in your case.

Municipal bonds are the "feel-good story" of bond investing because they generally stand for investments in state and local government projects that impact our daily lives. This includes highways, hospitals, housing, schools, and more. By investing in them, you're contributing to an improved quality of life for those around you (and yourself!). When you purchase a muni bond, you are loaning the issuing entity money, which will pay you a specified amount of interest and return the principal to you on a specified date of maturity. Having bonds insured guarantees that you'll get your money back, even if the municipality from which you bought them gets into financial difficulty and isn't able to pay you back on the agreed upon date. Almost half of all new issues are insured these days, signaling that investors are hungry for security.

Municipal bonds are bought and sold in the over-the-counter market, as opposed to trading on an exchange. About 2,700 banks and brokerage firms all over the United States are registered with the Municipal Securities Rulemaking Board (www.msrb.org) to buy and sell these bonds. They're bought, sold, and priced on the basis of credit quality, maturity, liquidity, and, most important for an investor, yield. Dealers in the municipal bond market compete with one another for customers based on yield and service, so to be sure you're getting the best price, search for daily price and yield information.

Leading Fixed-Income ETFs by Assets	Ticker	Total Assets (Millions)
iShares Lehman 1–3 Year Treasury Bond Fund	SHY	$9,517
iShares Lehman Aggregate Bond Fund	AGG	$7,738
Vanguard Intermediate-Term Bond	BIV	$7,211
Vanguard Short-Term Bond	BSV	$6,534
iShares Lehman TIPS Bond Fund	TIP	$5,299
Vanguard Long-Term Bond	BLV	$2,776
iShares Lehman 7–10 Year Treasury Bond Fund	IEF	$2,525
iShares Lehman 20+ Year Treasury Bond Fund	TLT	$1,487
iShares Lehman Short Treasury Bond Fund	SHV	$548
iShares S&P National Municipal Bond	MUB	$332

Federal Government Bonds

The debt securities that the U.S. Treasury, government agencies, and other government-sponsored enterprises (GSEs) issue are among the world's largest and most liquid. They're used to finance the debt of the federal government. Both GSEs and Treasury bonds make up less than 10 percent of all U.S. household bond investments.

U.S. Treasury securities are considered the safest of all investments because they are guaranteed by the U.S. government's "full faith and credit." For that reason, interest rates generally are lower than for other widely traded debt. That's how bonds are priced: generally, the lower the risk, the lower the rate. The amount of marketable U.S. Treasury securities is *enormous*: *about* $7 trillion in outstanding bills, notes, and bonds by the end of 2007. *Marketable securities* refers to securities that can trade on the open market. *Nonmarketable securities* include those that are not transferable, but that can be purchased from and redeemed by the government. Savings bonds are actually a form of nonmarketable security. You alone own your savings bonds—you cannot trade them with anyone else.

GSEs are financing entities created by Congress, such as Freddie Mac and Fannie Mae to fund loans to homeowners, farmers, and students. These bonds help the government address concerns about how members of these groups will be able to borrow enough money to meet their needs at rates they can afford.

The GSE-issued debt securities and programs, whether insured or guaranteed, offer investors a combination of high credit quality, liquidity, pricing transparency, and cash flow that is customized to mirror an investor's objective. On the flip side, GSEs demand that investors be educated and understand the price sensitivity and performance characteristics of what they're buying. Investors can't simply purchase these bonds and then forget about them—they need to monitor their performance continuously.

iMyth: TIPS Will Protect You Against Some Inflation

TIPS are not what you'd give your waiter for stellar service, but rather Treasury Inflation-Protected Securities (see www.treasurydirect.gov). Introduced in 1997, TIPS adjust their interest based on inflation. TIPS make good sense because deflation is rare. Prices seem to be going ever higher, and most economists say the historic rate of inflation is around 3 to 3.5 percent annually. Although the Treasury issues TIPS, the government also controls the inflation index used to determine how much its investors will actually get. That means the TIPS yield is set according to the Consumer Price Index, which is a conservative estimate of the cost of living. Nobody gets rich from buying TIPS, but they are a useful hedge against loss of purchasing power.

Corporate Bonds

Corporate bonds are just that: debts that industrial, financial, and service companies issue to finance capital investment and cash flow. They're I.O.U.s issued by both public and private companies, typically in multiples of $1,000. The funds raised are used to build facilities, buy necessary equipment, and otherwise help the business grow. How are they different from stocks? Simple—when you buy a bond, you are lending money, and you don't get an ownership interest in the company.

The market for corporate bonds is also bigger than the markets for municipal bonds, U.S. Treasury securities, and government agencies securities. Their popularity stems from their high yield (which also means the risk is greater—you can't get something for nothing); the reliable income stream they provide; the array of choices investors have when it comes to bond structures, coupon rates, maturity dates, credit quality, and industry exposure; and their marketability, meaning that if you need to sell your bond before it matures, you won't have much trouble finding a buyer. For well-capitalized corporations with excellent credit rating, the risk of default is quite remote.

Corporate bonds are typically divided into three groups:

- Short-term notes with maturities of up to 5 years
- Medium-term notes/bonds with maturities of 5 to 12 years
- Long-term bonds with maturities of more than 12 years and usually up to 30 years

If the investment-grade category of bonds are the top-shelf, AAA-rated bonds and others go down from there to BBB. Junk bonds, those with higher chances of default, are rated anywhere from BB down to D. Higher yields are paid for debentures, which are unsecured corporate bonds, so a highly rated company offering debentures will also pay a very competitive interest rate.

Companies that issue junk bonds pay high yields because they don't have any other choice. Their credit ratings are low, which makes it a challenge to get any capital at any cost. There are two kinds of junk bonds: fallen angels and rising stars. *Fallen angels* are just that: bonds that were once highly rated but have since been knocked back a few notches. *Rising stars* are bonds that are junk at the moment but are on their way to being investment quality. Junk bonds in any category, obviously, are risky.

Corporate bonds of any category carry risk, although the higher the rating, the safer they are. If a corporation files for bankruptcy, anyone who has some form of stake in the company—employees, shareholders, bondholders, or creditors—becomes very concerned about the future of the company. If you're a bondholder, your investment could be at risk. This does not mean you lose everything. Bondholders have *priority* of payment over common stockholders, meaning they get paid first. So even when a company is partially or fully liquidated, most bondholders get a portion of their equity back, at worst. In a reorganization, they could be made whole and lose nothing.

Bankruptcy generally means a company no longer can pay its debts when they're due. Filing bankruptcy gives a company a chance to reorganize its business so it can return to profitability with some of its debts forgiven or reduced, or completely liquidated, meaning selling off the assets to pay the debts.

Public companies can file for bankruptcy under either Chapter 7 or Chapter 11 of the federal bankruptcy laws. If the filing is under Chapter 7, the corporation is liquidated after the courts have determined that reorganizing wouldn't be worthwhile. If the filing is requested under Chapter 11, the company will continue to operate while reorganizing, but a bankruptcy court must approve all major business decisions.

Bonds represent a debt that a company has promised to repay with interest. When a company files for bankruptcy protection, bondholders have a better shot at getting their money back than the stockholders, due to the contractual priority of debt over equity. Bankruptcy laws determine the order of repayment, and stockholders are the last to have any claim on a company's assets.

Putting It All Together

Buying an ETF that tracks a bond index offers a low-cost and simple way to invest in bonds just as you would buy a single stock—that is, in one simple transaction.

If you're thinking about getting into bond ETFs, this can be a secure investment tool, as long as you do your homework. Bond ETFs offer some of the best diversification out there when it comes to investing in bonds. In addition, you get the combined diversification and liquidity because the ETF is traded on the public exchange rather than through an underwriter. The ETF is a fantastic way to get wide exposure to a market with considerable risk, but also with fantastic reward if it's played well.

Some of the risks include these:

- **Credit risk**—If a holding in a bond ETF defaults, it affects the price of the ETF. Fortunately, most fixed-income indexes have stable and high credit.

- **Interest rate risk**—When you buy a bond mutual fund or ETF, it's different than owning an individual bond. You can hold a bond to maturity and not suffer from fluctuations in the bond's value. When interest rates creep up, the value of the outstanding bonds tends to decline as new bonds with higher yields are issued. When rates decline, it's the reverse: Bonds currently on the market can appreciate in value because the new bonds don't offer as much interest. Thus, you see bonds traded at either a discount or a premium of face value. Because you would never hold a mutual fund or ETF to maturity like you would a single bond, they are all susceptible to interest rate risk and fluctuate right along with them. Buying and holding bond ETFs offers fluctuating yields. Their values are never guaranteed to remain stable.

Building a bond ETF comes with some challenges: The architect must be sure that it will closely track its underlying index in a way that remains cost-effective, considering the lack of liquidity in the bond market. Because most bonds are held until they've matured, an active secondary market isn't generally open to them, which makes it a real challenge to be sure a bond ETF has enough liquidity to track its index.

Exchange Traded Notes

A relative of the ETF that is somewhat new on the scene is the *exchange traded note* (ETN). They have similar names, trade daily on an exchange, offer short sales, and have similar expense ratios, but ETNs and ETFs part ways in their structure. ETNs are issued as senior bank notes (instead of an underlying index or commodity, as in the case of ETFs). This gives ETNs a measure of dependability.

ETNs have no tracking errors, and they comply with their underlying indexes minus the annual expense of 75 basis points a year. Barclays, the first issuer of ETNs, has suggested that investors treat them as prepaid contracts, meaning that any price difference between the sale and the purchase will be classified as capital gains. No other distributions come from ETNs.

Aside from the difference in their tax treatments, ETNs and ETFs differ in their risk profiles. ETNs come with a credit risk: If the bank or issuer behind them goes belly up, the holder of the note might not get the promised return. ETFs, on the other hand, have almost no credit risk, but there *is* the possibility that an ETF's returns will not match those of its underlying index.

Unfortunately, the IRS and the Treasury Department are questioning the favorable tax treatment of ETNs and have discussed doing away with their tax advantage altogether. Look out: Morningstar analyst Sonya Morris has said that if the IRS determines ETNs are just a means to avoid taxes, shareholders could be on the hook for back taxes. Ouch. If you're worried about that, Morris suggests keeping the notes in a tax-deferred account.

In December 2007, the IRS made one ruling regarding ETNs, at least: Any financial products linked to a single currency should be treated as debt for federal tax purposes—even if they are publicly listed on an exchange, as ETNs are.

The IRS has asked for industry comment on ETNs tracking commodities and stocks. If they hand down a similar decision to the one made on currency ETNs, observers say that it could deliver a blow to Barclays and other ETN providers. As of October 2007, Barclays sponsored 16 ETNs with $4 billion in assets.

Things are about to get very interesting, from the looks of it. Stay tuned.

iMoney Strategy: Buying Bond ETFs

If you're torn between buying bond ETFs and buying index bond funds, you should know that they generally experience similar performance. Bond ETFs are the better choices for investors seeking flexible trading and more transparency—you can find out what your portfolio looks like at any hour of the day online. With an index bond fund, that information is only available semiannually. How do the bond ETFs address the issue of liquidity? They use what's called "representative sampling," meaning that the fund tracks only a sufficient number of bonds to represent the entire index. The bonds in the sample are usually the largest and most liquid. As an example, the Lehman Aggregate Bond Index has more than 6,000 bonds, but the Barclays iShares Lehman Aggregate Bond Fund (AGG) has just a little more than 100 of those bonds. However, bond ETFs are recommended as part of a buy-and-hold strategy because they have a nasty tendency to rack up big trading commissions.

9

Retire with Dignity: The 401(e) Plan

The amount of funds invested in ETFs will ultimately equal the amount invested in mutual funds—sooner, perhaps, rather than later.

—ETF Investor Gerry D'Iteau

Mitch Anthony bobs and weaves through his presentation like a middleweight boxer. He's light on his feet, he's passionate, and his words carry punch; his delivery has a touch of evangelical zeal. Although his talks are largely geared toward financial advisors, he can articulate a vision of retirement perfectly customized to your needs.

"Don't think about retiring *from* something, but retiring *to* something," Anthony says. "In fact, you shouldn't think about retiring at all! While sipping martinis by the pool or playing golf five days a week may sound like a grand life right now, after a month or two, you'll wish you were back at the office. We've heard from scores of people who thought they wanted a life of ease but instead got a life of boredom."

Anthony encourages people to create "a vision of what you want your life to look like" as you go forward. Your life plan, however you design it, is something you'll need time to develop. If you already have one, great. How you get there is where ETFs might come into play.

Retirement isn't what it used to be. Traditionally, you put in your 30 years, happily attended your retirement party, and took home the gold watch. With fewer defined-benefit pensions now offered, a poor savings rate, and inefficient use of 401(k)-type plans, millions of Americans now work past 65. Welcome to what Anthony calls the *new retirementality*, also the title of one of his books. There is no template for this new prosperity. Want to work part-time when your career is over? Need to reinvent yourself after going back to school and taking up a new profession or trade? Want to start a business? Contract your services to your former employer as a consultant? According to the Employee Benefit Research Institute (www.ebri.org), the number of people 55 and older actively in the labor force increased from 38 percent in 1993 to 45 percent in 2006. The number of people ages 65 to 69 in the work force increased from about 18 percent in 1985 to 29 percent in 2006. In addition, the percentage of workers age 55 and older who work full-time increased from 54 percent in 1993 to 64 percent in 2005.

To make a big life-work change, though, you need to plan ahead and save diligently. These days, you have to work harder than ever for the privilege of retiring. That's right—retirement isn't something you're magically granted when you hit the magic age of 65. The day you leave the office for the last time is often decades in the making, the result of careful planning, faithful saving, and responsible investing. And the sooner you get started with your retirement planning, the more comfortable your Golden Years are apt to be.

A Reality Check

The days of fat company pensions are over, and Social Security is no longer a certainty. During World War II, 42 workers paid into Social Security for each person receiving benefits. By 2030, when most baby boomers will be retired, only *two* working people will contribute for each person receiving benefits. If you're a member of the post–baby boom generation, Social Security might not look the same as it has in the past.

Check out these numbers from the *Retirement Confidence Survey* from the Employee Benefit Research Institute:

- The proportion of workers saving for retirement has remained unchanged since 2001.
- Two-thirds of workers don't expect their standard of living to decline in retirement.
- Two in five workers say they're not willing to cut back on their spending to save for retirement.
- Four out of ten people aged 55 or older have less than $100,000 saved toward their retirement.
- More than three-quarters of those over age 55 have less than $100,000 in investable assets. Only 2 percent of Baby Boomers will receive an inheritance of more than $100,000.
- One out of four workers does not sign up for an employer's 401(k), and only one in ten contributes the maximum allowed.
- About half cash out their 401(k) savings when they change jobs instead of rolling over into an Individual Retirement Account (IRA) to avoid taxes.

But wait! It gets even worse: People are now living longer than ever. The U.S. Centers for Disease Control and Prevention (www.cdc. gov) reported in 2007 that the average U.S. lifespan is about 78 years. In any other context, that's good news, but not if you're inadequately prepared for retirement. In that case, it means that you have to save more for that longer life (and don't forget that higher cost of living).

In a September 2007 article for Voice of America, Robert Anderson of the National Center for Health Statistics revealed that longer life spans are part of a decades-long trend. "Over a century, life expectancies [have] increased, and I don't really have any reason to expect that it won't continue to do so."

Young people, especially, are on a collision course with disaster. Of those born in 1990, 37 percent will reach retirement age in the 2050s with *no savings at all,* according to a Government Accountability Office (www.gao.gov) report. And young workers just now entering the workforce will save enough in their 401(k)s to replace only 22 percent of their preretirement income. As of December 2007, the median 401(k) account balance for all workers was $22,800.

Among workers aged 55 to 64, the median in 2004 was $50,000. That's enough to provide an annual income of $4,400 a year. The picture is bleak, indeed.

Boomers May Go Bust

Allow us to be blunt: Whether you're 22 or 62, you can't afford to ignore your financial life plan. If you haven't started saving for retirement, what are you waiting for? As the next generation in line for retirement, however, the 77 million members of the Baby Boom generation (those born between 1946 and 1964) have a lot to think about. The crisis is no longer far off in the future. It's now. Our financial system is unprepared for the onslaught of people entering their retirement years, and it's more imperative than ever for retirees to be prepared to take care of themselves instead of relying on a system that could well fail.

The first wave of Baby Boomers is qualified for Social Security right now. They're thinking about putting to use the money they've amassed in their IRAs or from sales of their homes or stock options.

What about the average lifespan? That number is a bit misleading, too. More than half of 65-year-olds will reach age 85. Another 18 percent will live to between 90 and 94. That's a lot of retirement savings to amass.

Of those over 65, 48 percent will need nursing home care. That's not a surprise. But what is a surprise is this: Only 6 percent of consumers own long-term care policies!

Even if you're not a member of the Baby Boom generation, it's important to realize that things will not improve much for you.

Black Box Retirement Plans: Costs Are Not Transparent

When the American Association of Retired Persons (www.aarp. org), a nonprofit group for folks over 50 (John has received his card in the mail), conducted a survey asking, "How much are you being charged for your 401(k) plan?" 80 percent said they had no idea. That's a huge problem because the 401(k) is the primary U.S. retirement vehicle, serving more than 45 million Americans. It was never meant to pull the lion's share of the retirement savings load; it was originally designed as a supplemental plan. But with the gradual disappearance of the defined-benefit or "traditional" pension (big companies such as IBM are simply not offering them anymore), the 401(k) and its sisters 457 and 403(b) programs are the only retirement vehicle for most employees.

The good news is that, in late 2007, Congress and the U.S. Department of Labor approved plans that automatically enroll you in a 401(k)-type plan when you start with a new employer that offers them. Keep in mind, though, that employers are not required to offer these plans, so 40 percent of the American workforce, mostly employed by small businesses, have no pension plan at all. Autoenrollment means that you must opt out of a plan when you are hired. Because most workers are unlikely to do that, savings rates should skyrocket as payroll deductions are directed to a default investment mix of mutual funds. With your retirement funding on autopilot, it's out of sight and out of mind. No more thinking about how much to save or where to put it. The best-designed plans will do the thinking for you.

The downside of the modern 401(k) is that it's still a black box. Because it's a package of mutual funds managed and administered by third parties, you have no idea how much you're paying in total expenses. Middlemen can pass along expenses that are buried in "expense ratios" of the funds within your plan. That's money you can't afford to lose, so urge your employer to bring in a transparent, low-cost plan using ETFs.

Most investor ownership of ETFs has occurred outside of retirement plans, but ETFs in retirement plans make perfect sense because the expenses are low and it's an attractive thing for aging investors. In addition, it is the trend of the future.

---

iMyth: What You See Is What You Get in 401(k)s

The U.S. Government Accountability Office found that most 401(k) participants think they aren't paying *any* fees. That's troublesome because expenses eat up returns over time. Paying 1 percent in 401(k) expenses will reduce your retirement fund by 17 percent over 20 years and 30 percent over 30 years. Expenses are generally hidden in *expense ratios*, the percentage of your funds taken by middlemen every year. So a 1 percent expense ratio (it should be half that in a cost-efficient plan) will nip $1,000 of your hard-earned money every year if you have $100,000. Where does this money go? You might never know because disclosure is not required. You can demand this information of your employer. After all, it's your money. Ask how much you are paying in 12(b)1, administration, fund management, commissions, trading expenses, subtransfer, and website expenses. All of these fees are negotiable, of course, but *you* can't do the work to lower expenses (unless you own your own company and manage the retirement plan). Is your 401(k) wrapped within a variable annuity structure? Try to get out of it because it's the most expensive way of packaging a 401(k). Your employer is charged with prudently managing your plan. Under federal law, they must provide the best plan at the lowest cost. Hold them to it. It's your money.

The Next Step: The 401(e)

ETFs are a new and viable path to retirement savings. By offering low cost and diversification, they can be a wise and versatile vehicle on which you can ride into retirement. We call ETF-based retirement plans the *401(e)*.

Until early 2007, most of the growth in ETFs took place outside the realm of 401(k)s, but retirement plan sponsors are actively exploring the different ways ETFs can be incorporated into this mutual fund-heavy area. As a retired investor, there is no longer any reason you have to be on the outside looking in with ETFs—if you feel prepared to invest in them.

Until recently, ETFs were considered incompatible with 401(k) plans and were not considered savvy investments for someone a few years away from retirement. A few years ago, they were rarely featured in an investor's retirement plan. After all, the 401(k) model is one in which an investor puts money in, lets it sit in mutual funds and accrue interest over a period of years, and then takes out and enjoys the funds. ETFs, on the other hand, are bought and sold like stock.

No one template for retirement exists anymore. Some choose to work part-time. Others go the nonprofit route. And because life-long learning is a great idea for anyone, many choose to go back to school or start a new career—or two. No matter which route you choose, you will need the financial flexibility to pursue it. That's where our iMoney strategies come in; we will help you get to where you need to be.

ETFs Offer New Alternatives to Investing

Safer investing alternatives are slowly becoming available for investors who are keeping one eye on their retirement years. There are fixed-income and bond ETFs, which cover a variety of markets, including the Treasury, corporate mixed security markets, and more. They're not just for those investors with retirement around the corner. To be sure, the sooner you start thinking about these funds, the better. It doesn't do as much good to get into them five years out of retirement as it does 30 years before the big day.

Most plan providers in the United States won't offer ETFs because they are concerned about intraday trading. The fees that result from switching your holdings in and out will swiftly diminish, if not entirely cancel out, any gains you might have. This isn't good for the health and longevity of you *or* your retirement plan. Also, unlike mutual funds, ETFs don't allow you to add small amounts of money each month without incurring those fees. Dollar cost averaging doesn't make a lick of sense at $20 per transaction, does it? Some new alternatives are worth exploring, however.

401(e) Providers Use New Technology

The introduction of ETFs into 401(k) plans didn't come easy. For one, the big mutual fund companies are also 401(k) providers, and they didn't have much incentive to find a way to incorporate them into plans that they managed. Mutual funds make their money in fees. They have dominated 401(k) plans as the ultimate buy-and-hold tool for workers saving for retirement. It's a passive approach, but it's a safe one.

But some problems have arisen within the 401(k) market. There's not much professional investment advice out there for individuals in the workplace. Employers are the plan sponsors, and they tend to like 401(k)s because they're cheaper than traditional pension plans.

Instead of keeping up a pension portfolio for their employees, employers shift the onus for asset allocation to their employees, and many of those employees are not savvy enough to manage a financial portfolio of retirement savings. Those employees wind up putting large chunks of their portfolio in their company's stock or other funds and don't consider the importance of diversifying, according to landmark research by economists Richard Thaler, a professor at the University of Chicago, and Schlomo Benartzi, a professor at UCLA. Employees don't keep an eye on allocations or recalibrate their portfolios even when the markets have changed.

Enter the Pension Protection Act of 2006, offering hope that ETFs would soon be incorporated into 401(k) plans. Among other things, it states that if there is enough investor interest in ETFs as part of pension plans, employers have a fiduciary duty to provide that option.

But before they could be officially incorporated into any plans, providers must clear one major hurdle: They need an automated system to accommodate both ETFs and mutual funds. The old system was designed to handle only the latter, which are priced at the end of the day. Throw continually priced ETFs into the mix, and you've got a math problem only a computer (and possibly Albert Einstein) could solve.

Darwin Abrahamson, founder and CEO of Invest n Retire (www.investnretire.com), in Portland, Oregon, said in 2005, "Many believe the big hurdle for ETFs and 401(k) plans is commissions." Abrahamson ultimately found the solution with a software package designed to manage ETFs in 401(k) plans. The software is the result of years of work, and it finally launched in January 2007 with, Abrahamson says, a lot of success.

Invest n Retire offers 30 Barclays Global Investors iShares ETFs, NASDAQ ETFs, 13 Vanguard VIPERs, and 18 Dimensional Fund Advisors funds in about 25 retirement plans, with assets ranging from $1 million to $10 million. By using ETFs, he says, his firm has significantly reduced costs of managing 401(k) plans, resulting in expenses 30 to 60 percent below the plans that conventional 401(k) service providers offer. And because Abrahamson's software does rebalancing, it is accomplished daily—something that would be prohibitively expensive otherwise.

The software has given the market for ETFs in 401(k) plans a big boost. Abrahamson is optimistic about the future of ETFs in retirement plans. "Over the next two to three years, we will see huge inflows of ETF assets into 401(k) plans."

The absence of the proper software wasn't the only holdup to ETFs entering the 401(k) market. Mike Hatlee, head of the retirement services group at Chemung Canal Trust (www.chemungcanal. com), proposes that a 401(k) for ETFs needs to feature high trading volume, substantial assets, and a large number of participants so that trading costs can be spread out.

401(e) Candidates: Top Index ETFs By Assets	Ticker	Total Assets (Millions)
Vanguard Total Stock Market	VTI	$106,385
SPDRs	SPY	$98,153
iShares MSCI EAFE Index	EFA	$51,896
Vanguard European Stock	VGK	$36,143
iShares MSCI Emerging Markets Index	EEM	$28,854
Vanguard Emerging Markets Stock	VWO	$24,690
PowerShares QQQ	QQQQ	$21,767
Vanguard Mid-Cap	VO	$20,756
iShares S&P 500 Index	IVV	$17,895
Vanguard Growth	VUG	$17,063

Not for Everyone

Gus Sauter, managing director of the Vanguard Core Management Group, is not a fan of incorporating ETFs into retirement plans. In an interview with Vanguard's *ETFs In Focus* publication, he came out strongly against them. "I'm quite skeptical about ETFs being a popular option in 401(k) plans. We've done a wealth of analysis on 401(k) plans...and find that participants become frozen in the headlights when you offer too many options."

Not everyone has been sour on the idea of ETFs entering the retirement plan arena; some see the change as a welcome one. Mutual fund fees are higher than those of ETFs, and stocks are projected to average returns in the single digits for the next few years. The ETF-based plan, which represents a scant 3 percent of the $3 trillion 401(k) market, won't catch on unless total expenses make this idea competitive with traditional models.

Several providers are working to offer 401(k) plans to include ETFs. Beginning in June 2007, retirement plan provider BenefitStreet began offering ETFs on its 401(k) platform in conjunction with Barclays Global Investors. Barclays has worked with several retirement plans and has found that the technology is finally making enough advancement to offer ETFs within retirement plans. ShareBuilder is another 401(k) provider offering ETFs in its plan.

The way most 401(e) vendors get around the persistent commission costs in buying ETFs—remember, you're charged a commission every time you buy and sell an ETF—is through bunching up trades or what's known as "aggregated orders at the fund level," getting huge discounts on transaction fees. Keep in mind that although ETF-based plans are much lower cost than traditional 401(k)s, there are expenses involved. ShareBuilder, for example, charges an "implementation" fee up to $995, plus administration fees up to $200 per month (at time of publication). Expense ratios on the ETFs within the plan range from .22 to .49 percent annually. ShareBuilder also levies .75 percent in annual management.

Most experts agree that if ETFs want to be big players in the 401(k) market, the transaction/brokerage costs will have to decline, investors will need to get more familiar with ETFs, and the ETF industry will have to convince people that they present an attractive retirement asset.

ETFs with an Expiration Date

In October 2007, XShares Advisors and RPG Consultants teamed up to make it possible for plan sponsors, advisors, brokers, and third-party administrators to add ETFs into their retirement plan portfolios. A month later, in November, RPG announced that it would provide a platform allowing financial advisors to offer XShares' family of target-date ETFs as the default option in 401(k) plans.

XShares Group CEO Bill Henson says the target date funds, which automatically rebalance according to the date they "expire" as a person nears retirement, are a "lower-cost, one-step solution to retirement planning." This move eliminates many of the providers' concerns that putting ETFs in 401(k) plans is a cost-prohibitive venture.

Leading Vendors of ETF-Based Retirement Plans

Fortunately, you have a choice of vendors when setting up a 401(e). Here's a short list of companies offering 401(k) plans employing ETFs:

- Benefit Street (www.benefitstreet.com)
- Invest n Retire (www.investnretire.com)
- ShareBuilder (www.sharebuilder401k.com)
- Wisdom Tree (www.wisdomtree.com)
- XTF Advisors (www.xtf.com)

ETFs in Your IRA Accounts

It isn't imperative to have ETFs in tax-advantaged accounts such as 401(k)s, but if you're a frequent trader, it makes more sense to do it in an IRA. Of course, you will still be on the hook for commission costs, although your trading activity will be sheltered from income taxes until you withdraw the money.

If you're a fan of small-cap ETFs, for example, it could be another shrewd reason to include ETFs in your IRA. Because small-caps generally have higher turnover rates than large-caps—primarily because holdings that have grown too big need to be sold—you can realize gains. Likewise, if you're into the more exotic ETFs, such as commodities, a tax-deferred account might be your best alternative. That's because as your commodity ETF closes old futures contracts and enters into new ones, 40 percent of those gains are subject to short-term capital gains taxes, which don't apply in the tax-deferred IRA account.

As for bond ETFs, conventional wisdom is that bond funds should be kept in tax-sheltered accounts because of the high yields they offer. Bond income is not subject to the low capital gains rate (15 percent or lower), so placing them in a tax-deferred account makes sense. But perhaps the best place for your equity and fixed-income investments depends on how long you have to go until you retire and what you figure your tax bracket will be at that time. The longer you have to go and the lower your tax bracket, the more you'll want to keep your stocks in a retirement account and your bonds in a taxable account.

And We Come Full Circle

Our whole discussion inevitably winds up back where we started in this book: with the mutual fund scandals of the early 2000s. Some of the investors who went through it and lost big money still had some time to recover from the hit. Their portfolios rebounded and, in the end, they were all right. But what about those who were close to retiring? They didn't have the luxury of a nice distance from quitting time that they could use to slowly but surely rebuild and rise from the ashes.

Investors closing in on retirement who remember the bad days are inclined to be even more cautious today. For years, planning for long-term growth meant shifting to bonds when you retired. Individual bonds are easy. They're generally safe and reliable. They won't blow up in your face. So what's the problem with bonds? Well, although you'll get a fixed income from them, there are other risks. Except for Treasury Inflation-Protected Securities (TIPS), they aren't indexed to inflation. And when interest rates or inflation tick up, bonds lose value. Unless they are issued by the U.S. Treasury or a highly rated corporation, they come with credit risk. Switching over to ETFs can bring in more money while still giving you a safety net with transparency and higher liquidity.

Consider this frightening scenario: What if the market dives shortly after you retire? Hey, it could happen. Look at the year 2000, or October 1987, or the late 1970s and early 1980s. It could be your own bad luck if it happened just as you are preparing to head into your new prosperity. You can always insulate your portfolio by buying TIPS or Certificates of Deposit (CDs), if you're looking for absolute security. With the growth portion of your portfolio, diversification is the key.

Incorporating an ETF into your retirement portfolio doesn't necessarily bind you to being either conservative or risky. There is a gray area in there, too, in which you can divvy it up a bit. Put a little bit of money into ETFs that are viewed as slightly riskier—commodities or currencies, for example—and put the remainder of your money into more conservative ETFs. One thing is for certain: You will have a better return going the ETF route than waiting for those bonds to mature.

iMoney Strategy: Building a Secure 401(e)

If you think adding ETFs to your 401(k) plan is wise, you still have some things to consider. Not every plan is well suited to the addition of an ETF, and if you are in or coming up on retirement, you need to consider what the future might hold and make the decision based on your individual goals and personal risk tolerance. Here are ten things to think about regarding ETFs in your retirement plan before taking the plunge:

1. **Direct ownership**—You should own shares of ETFs directly in your plan to avoid the expense of establishing a self-directed brokerage account and to avoid additional fees of ETFs held in a collective trust (a fund created by pooling investments by institutional investors), mutual fund, or managed account.

2. **Total expenses**—What is your return after all fees are deducted?

3. **Manager background**—Check the track record of the manager of the collective trust, fund, or separately managed account (an account tailored to your specific needs) offering ETFs.

4. **The fine print**—If you're investing in a collective trust, be sure to request fact sheets and the paperwork required to open an account—and *then read it.*

5. **The prospectus**—If the investment option is a mutual fund, request and read the prospectus and annual report.

6. **SEC disclosure statements**—If the investment option is a separately managed account, request the Form ADV disclosure statement. (See www.sec.gov/answers/formadv.htm for more information.)

7. **Individual share requirements**—Do you need to own individual shares of an ETF to open a self-directed brokerage account? If so, ask about commissions, daily trading, and how often the trades are placed.

8. **How trading is handled**—Does the 401(k) provider place all the trades with a brokerage firm or net buys and sells in an internal account? Check with your financial advisor to avoid any conflicts of interest.

9. **Separate accounts**—Is there a separate custodial account for each plan, or does the 401(k) commingle all plan assets in a single brokerage account? Each qualified plan must hold its assets in a separate custodial or trust account. Commingling assets with other qualified plans is against the law.

10. **Tools provided**—What tools does the 401(k) provider offer participants to help in selecting an asset-allocation plan? Do your homework.

10

Hedging Your Bets: Long and Short ETFs

The increasing restrictions (exit fees if held less than 90 days for many funds) and high fees led me to ETFs. Many actively managed funds do not do as well as their ETF counterparts (probably because of inexperienced managers—and those fees). I do have some single-company stocks, but [I] like ETFs for most of our investments because of the diversification this affords at a much lower price than it would cost to get that same diversification with single-company stocks.

—Joe Darrow, ETF investor

Joe Darrow has discovered what institutional investors learned years ago. To own huge swaths of the market, you have to turn off the active management jingle that Wall Street hums 24 hours a day. You buy index funds for diversification. The reason is simple. The more securities you own, the lower your exposure is to any one stock or bond. There's safety in holding large numbers of securities, and if you stray from the herd, you get into trouble. Remember Lucent, Cisco, and Global Crossing from their heydays in the late 1990s? What happened to them in 2001? Millions were betting that these companies would lead the way in technology. Although they might have been innovators, they were wildly overvalued, and investors who loaded up on them got scorched.

At the height of the dotcom bubble, John was approached by a friend, who wanted to get in on the eye-popping frenzy of the late 1990s. "Should I buy Cisco?" the friend asked him. "Absolutely not," John replied. "It's way overpriced, and this rally can't go on much longer. Buy an index fund."

You would've thought John had told his friend to go get a root canal without anesthesia. Sure enough, the market collapsed—and John's friend still bought the stock. "I should have listened to you," he later said.

What would have made sense at the time—and saved investors trillions of dollars—was the equivalent of watching grass grow. Wallflower index funds were *not* the vehicle of choice for most investors. Millions preferred to listen to tipsters on television or radio, or, worse yet, their brothers-in-law. They were sold on what they knew, which meant name brand stocks. Yet where's the logic of investing in single companies when you have more than 10,000 other companies to choose from and you can own them through ETFs? Better yet, suppose you heeded all the warning signs that the market was going to take a dive and you did something about it? When the stock market falters and stumbles, your portfolio is like the captain going down with the ship. The whole point of investing in the market is to *make* money, not *lose* it.

So what's an investor to do if there's a giant bear storming through the markets? Cash out, hide somewhere, and wait until the bull comes back, right? Wrong! You can capitalize on market downturns and even make them work in your favor.

The Hedging Strategy

Most investors don't have to sit back or ride anything out. As you gain access to additional information about investing, you begin to feel more comfortable venturing into more exotic territories. You can take a proactive approach to protecting your money, venturing into the world of long and short ETFs.

The idea behind long-short investing is pretty simple: You're just taking advantage of the dips and downturns of the market. In a perfect world, of course, the market would be going up all the time and investing would be cut-and-dry. The world isn't perfect, which could be the universe's way of keeping things interesting. The market rises and falls; it sways from side to side. It always has, always will. Just as with the peaks and valleys of life, you have a choice: You can take an acceptance approach and gamely go along for the ride, come what may, or you can be proactive and turn lemons into lemonade.

Short-selling is a tricky and risky strategy in which you profit from a stock going south. It involves borrowing stock and then selling it, hoping that it will decrease in value so that you can buy it back at a lower price and keep the difference. Confused? Read on....

Say Company A's stock sells for $20 a share. As a short seller, you believe that the shares are going to drop in price, so you borrow 100 shares and then sell them for $2,000. If the share price drops as anticipated and Company A's stock is now selling for $10 a share, you can buy them for $1,000 and close the short position, then return the shares to their original owner and make a nice little profit of $1,000. The "original owner" in most short sales is your broker, who also charges you interest on the shares you borrow, adding interest cost to the strategy.

Of course, you could lose big time, too. If your hunch was way off and the price of Company A's shares goes *up* to $25, you have to buy those shares at $2,500 to close the short position, losing $500.

Short Selling's Dark History

Short selling has a bit of a tarnished history. Short selling was partly blamed for the Wall Street crash of 1929, and in 1940, mutual funds actually were banned from short selling. That law was eventually repealed in 1997. In 1949, Alfred Winslow Jones founded an unregulated fund that bought stocks while selling other stocks short, hedging some of the market risk; this gave rise to the hedge fund.

Mass short selling often occurs when market bubbles occur—for example, the dotcom bubble. Whenever there's frenzy in a particular sector, short sellers hope for a market downturn on which they can capitalize. And those corrections might eventually arrive. Bad news about a company is also an enticement to investors to sell a stock short.

Short sellers are typically investors who take a fundamentally negative or "bearish" view of the markets. They turn the old "buy low and sell high" adage on its head. Day traders and hedge funds are particularly fond of using short-selling profit on stocks that they believe are overvalued. Even if you're more Pollyanna than Scrooge, there's still a place for you in the short-selling market. Suspecting that something is going to head downward doesn't mean you're a pessimist—it just means you are aware that the markets are always changing and evolving. Things go up, things go down, things go back up, and so on. It's just being realistic.

Short Selling Beyond Stocks

Short selling goes beyond the world of stocks. It can be applied in nearly any segment of the market, including futures and currencies. Short selling with futures contracts means you have a legal obligation to deliver the commodity when the contract delivery day arrives. If you hold the short position, however, you can buy the contract before it expires to close the position. The producers of that commodity often use short futures transactions to fix the future price of goods they haven't made yet.

Selling short a currency isn't like selling stocks short. Currencies are traded in pairs, each currency priced in comparison with another. A contract is *always* long one position and short another. Consider an example:

Say you want to trade between with the U.S. dollar and the Euro, and the current market rate is $1= €;.50. You borrows €;1. With that, you have bought $2. The next morning, you wake up to learn that the Euro has gone up in value to €;.55. You sell your $2 and get €;1.10. You then give back the €;1 and keep the €;.10 profit.

Neat, right?

Selling Short with ETFs

Because ETFs are traded like stock on exchanges, they can also be sold short. They also have certain advantages over short-selling stocks: They are exempt from the up-tick rule that individual stocks face. Also known as the *short sale rule*, this is an SEC regulation stating that short sales can be made only in rising markets. This is to prevent raiders from selling short to drive a stock's price down.

Why get involved with shorting ETFs? For one thing, with ETFs, you have the alternative of shorting them even if the market is already on a downward trend. Instead of waiting for a stock to trade above its last executed price, you can short the shares at the next available bid and immediately enter the short position. If you were working with single-issue stocks, you would be unable to enter the short position because of the up-tick rule.

Long-short and leveraged ETFs offer distinct investment strategies during volatile times:

- Leveraged ETFs can give more market exposure with less capital. During the bull market of the 1990s, being able to put 10 percent of your portfolio in the market while experiencing twice the potential upside equated to having 20 percent of your portfolio allocated. ETFs are a great tool to target areas of the market that are experiencing positive momentum.

- Inverse leveraged ETFs act as an excellent hedge when the market finally turns. If you have low-cost basis stock positions and you are concerned about generating capital gain taxes if you sell, short/leveraged ETFs enable you to protect a portion of your portfolio without incurring the tax consequences of selling.

iMyth: You Can't Short the Housing Market

Another reason you might be attracted to shorting ETFs is that you believe a particular sector is about to see a downward trend. Just as sector ETFs do away with the necessity of choosing *which* stocks will go up or down and instead allow an investor to zero in on a sector overall, shorting ETFs enables you to choose a general segment of the market you foresee slowing down. An example might be the housing market in 2006. Home prices were skyrocketing, and people were clamoring to get on the train. Average homes were going for a million dollars or more in some markets. But that kind of trend can't possibly continue forever, right? By 2007, the upward trend had stalled. Suddenly, homes weren't selling, and if they were selling, many were not getting close to what they were asking. Those willing to buy homes were having a hard time getting the loans they needed to complete the transaction. It was a big, ugly mess.

Want to bet against Boston and go long on Los Angeles? Like all trading strategies, it's loaded with risk, but it can be done. MacroMarkets, LLC, has developed home price indexes for Boston, Chicago, Denver, Las Vegas, Los Angeles, Miami, New York, San Diego, San Francisco, and Washington, D.C. The indexes are tied to futures contracts listed on the Chicago Mercantile Exchange. As with any other commodities contracts, they are complicated and require a great deal of study before you consider them.

Trading Strategies

Now that you know the basics of selling short, we'll let you in on a secret: That isn't all there is to it. You might have had a hunch, considering that there never seems to be *just* one simple little way of doing things. For every investment alternative, there are a dozen variations of it, and naturally, this holds true for short investing, too. With short selling ETFs, there are three additional ways to go beyond the basic model: inverse, ultra, and ultrashort.

In 2006, ProShares launched a new line of ETFs that not only allowed investors to get ETFs doing the opposite of whatever the market did, but also some leveraged ETFs that did *twice* the opposite of whatever the market did. For example, if you had an inverse ETF for the S&P 500, then if the S&P went up 1 percent, your ETF would go down 1 percent, and vice versa. With an ultrashort, if the S&P went up 1 percent, your ETF would go down 2 percent and, again, vice versa. Ultra simply does whatever the market does times two: The S&P goes up 2 percent. The ultra goes up 4 percent. Call it the stock market's very own version of "double down." As you can see, the potential exists for an investor to do very, very well—or to flame out in a most spectacular fashion. Rydex Investments has since entered the fray with its own line of inverse ETFs, which launched in November 2007.

The ProShares line offers short or magnified exposure to a range of well-known indexes, covering everything from small-, mid-, and large-cap indexes and at least 11 sectors.

How Margin Accounts Work: Some Pitfalls

If your dream ETF is out there and you want to buy a lot of it, yet you can't afford it, what are you to do? Easy—you head to your broker and open a margin account, and you're in business. Boiled down to its simplest terms, a *margin account* is a means by which you borrow money to make investments you normally wouldn't be able to make. It isn't as simple as it sounds, of course, because as in any kind of situation in which someone is being loaned money, the lender wants to make sure he's actually going to get his money back.

The typical initial minimum investment for a margin account is at least $2,000, but some brokerages require even more. This initial deposit is referred to as the minimum margin. When your account is open for business, you can borrow up to 50 percent of the purchase price of a stock (the initial margin).

When you sell the stock in your margin account, proceeds go to your broker to repay the amount of the loan. You also must maintain a minimum account balance; otherwise, you can expect a margin call from your broker asking you to either deposit more money or sell some holdings. Probably the only thing less fun than that is getting a call from the credit card company asking where your payment might be. In volatile markets, you can expect to be asked to pony up quite a few times. And if you can't get above the maintenance margin, your broker has the right to sell your securities to get you there—and your broker is not required to consult you first.

With your margin account, you get a specific amount of buying power, depending on what you initially put into your account. For example, say you deposit $20,000 into your margin account. Because you put up 50 percent of the purchase price, you now have $40,000 of buying power. If you buy $5,000 of equities, you still have $35,000 left to spend, and you haven't even tapped into your margin. The borrowing officially begins only when you start buying securities worth more than $20,000. If the securities held in your account go up or down in value, this changes the amount of buying power you have.

The Federal Reserve Board decides which stocks are marginable. Pretty much anything in the penny stock, Over the Counter Bulletin Board (OTCBB), or initial public offerings (IPOs) cannot be bought on margin because those stocks are considered risky enough as it is.

Beyond that, it is left up to the individual brokerage to decide which stocks are marginable.

Warning: Over time, a margin account can be hazardous to your investment health. The debt increases as the interest accrues. And the interest accrues because your debt increases. If you're not careful, you could find yourself in a very deep hole before long. For this reason, margin accounts are best used for short-term investments. The longer you hold an investment, the more you need to earn just to break even—never mind ending up in the black.

Leading Long/Short Hedge ETFs	Ticker	Total Assets (Millions)
ProShares UltraShort S&P 500	SDS	$1,652
ProShares UltraShort QQQ	QID	$1,256
ProShares UltraShort Financials	SKF	$967
ProShares Ultra QQQ	QLD	$893
ProShares UltraShort Russell2000	TWM	$604
ProShares UltraShort Real Estate	SRS	$580
ProShares Ultra S&P 500	SSO	$568
ProShares UltraShort Dow30	DXD	$444
ProShares Ultra Dow30	DDM	$236
ProShares Short S&P 500	SH	$205
ProShares UltraShort MidCap400	MZZ	$160
Rydex Inverse 2x S&P 500	RSW	$16
Rydex Inverse 2x S&P MidCap400	RMS	$12
Rydex Inverse 2x Russell 2000	RRZ	$12

iMoney Strategy: Be Careful Out There

Of course, if you've got an itch you need to scratch and you've just got to get in on them, short ETFs can be a great alternative when you want to get short exposure in a convenient package. Short ETFs can work for certain retirement accounts where short selling isn't allowed. They're appropriate as long as you understand them, know the risks, and are looking to use the peaks and valleys of the market to their fullest extent. As long-term investments, they're not ideal because you will be fighting an uphill battle buying short ETFs and hanging on to them.

You can use short ETFs for hedging an entire portfolio or focusing on a particular sector. If you know all the caveats, yet you still can't resist, go ahead and invest in short ETFs. Just remember that they can turn on you on a dime, and be sure to have a stop-loss in place that—and this is key—you'll stick to when things begin to head in the wrong direction. Also, be particularly careful with margin trading. A big attraction of these accounts is the fact that if the markets go up, your earnings will be equally great. You can buy more than you'd ordinarily be able to with just the cash you possess, so your potential for success is magnified. But it bears repeating with a double-edge sword technique as this one: Buying on margin is the *only* stock-based investment where you can lose more than you invested. Therefore, it's wise to invest only what you can safely afford to lose. Proceed with caution, indeed, if you proceed at all.

With ETFs (as well as with other types of securities), you have what's known as *options*, which allow you to buy or sell a security at some point in the future. They're divvied up into two categories: calls and puts. Calls increase in value when the underlying security is also on the rise, and vice versa. They give you the right to buy a stock from the investor who sold you the call option at a specific price on or before a predetermined date. For example, if you agree to buy a stock on or before the last Monday of June at a "strike price" of $40, and the price of that stock rises above your agreed-upon amount, you're buying the stock for less than its market value. And if you don't want to buy the stock, you can sell it to someone else and make a tidy profit.

Meanwhile, puts increase in value when the security is going down and decrease as it's going up. A put gives you the right to sell a stock to the investor who sold you the put option at a specific price, on or before an agreed-upon date. As an example, if you bought a put option on a stock on January 1, it would come with terms that you could sell it for $35 before January 31. If the stock falls *below* that amount anytime before the expiration date, you can sell it for more than its market value and, once again, make some money.

The thing to remember is that both calls and puts come with an expiration date, and if you don't exercise your option before your date, you could lose it all. Nobody wants that.

11

What Lies Ahead: The Future of ETFs

The way I see it, this is the best thing to happen to mutual funds in 60 years. It is a complete (and overdue) modernization of a great concept. With the advent of active ETFs, the upgrade will be complete.

—Lee Edgcomb, ETF Trends reader

A friend of Tom's lives and works in Silicon Valley. As he approaches 50, he is about to embark on another high-tech growth company. Over the years, he has been a successful engineer and has benefited from the growth of the companies he's been involved in via their stock plans. At the same time, he has maxed out his 401(k) plan annually.

However, he seems to find comfort in keeping a handful of 401(k) accounts that have been legacies from past employers. "When I asked him about their allocation or performance he really couldn't recall but still felt comfort in their performance," Tom says. "There is a perceived diversification with accounts still being held at different custodians, even though there is no clear investment plan." There are millions of investors like him, but as they approach retirement, their attitudes about their 401(k) accounts change.

As baby boomers head into retirement, their 401(k) plans will mean more to them than ever. And although we've enjoyed the forced savings, tax benefits, and market growth they've provided, 401(k) plans deserve more attention. Americans seem too busy to take the time to maximize the benefits of the one thing that could make the difference between an okay retirement and a fantastic retirement.

Expect to see more tools and services that help you aggregate your retirement accounts. If multiple retirement accounts could be looked at as one, they would get much more attention. The tools will include allocation recommendations along with risk, planning, cost, and performance analysis. And when you are in a position to see the bottom-line numbers, ETFs will naturally make their way into 401(k) plans as investment options. In the end, you will demand more and get it.

Enter the Actively Managed ETF

By now, you've probably gleaned that we don't particularly like active mutual fund management as a strategy for most investors. Over time, most pros can't beat market averages consistently. So it might seem a bit counterintuitive and perhaps even a bit *loco* to have actively managed ETFs, doesn't it?

After all this talk about the advantages of ETFs over traditional mutual funds—one of which is the fact that because they *aren't* generally actively managed, the costs are significantly lower and those savings are passed on to investors—suddenly mutual funds are talking about adding ETFs into the mix that do just that.

Would an actively managed ETF give investors all the benefits of a managed mutual fund, with all the flexibility of an ETF? Can they can have their cake and eat it, too? The prospect of such a fund is likely to send shrieks of glee echoing throughout the world of investing.

Many ETF experts feel that the time is right for actively managed ETFs. As investment tools, they're getting more sophisticated all the time. Now that people are beginning to understand them, they want to see how far they can push the envelope with them. In the existing batch of ETFs, several funds already blur the lines between active and passive management. It's as though providers are testing the waters, feeling out investors before going whole hog.

The Cubes, Diamonds, and Spiders, for instance, are ETFs based on indexes that change little in composition. If ETFs were pizza, they'd be the plain cheese—simple, classic, and appealing to all (unless you're lactose intolerant, which is really too bad). The ETFs tracking them are on the passive end of the spectrum. Getting into the pepperoni pizza territory, there's the First Trust DB Strategic Value Index Fund (FDV), a tiny, little-known fund that veers into active management territory because it is reconstituted every month. It tracks a Deutsche Bank index that selects 40 of the cheapest-trading, largest capitalization stocks on the S&P 500 based on their PE ratios. Maintaining the look and feel of an actively managed fund has served FDV very well: Between its launch in 2006 and the middle of 2007, the fund returned 29 percent.

A better-known fund that shares a resemblance with the active management concept is the PowerShares FTSE RAFI U.S. 1000 (PRF). As we mentioned earlier, the RAFI fund is a fundamental index, weighting its holdings based on sales, dividends, book value, and income. The fund resembles active management because its construction departs from the typical market cap structure that index funds typically use. Since its launch in 2005 until the middle of 2007, the fund returned 18.4 percent. It is rebalanced once yearly with a turnover ratio of 8 percent, something which is expensive to do and sets off taxable gains. It's an intriguing fund, but you should weigh the pros and the cons carefully.

That brings us to the fully loaded pizza (sans pineapple, because some of us feel that pineapple on pizza is about as wrong as popcorn-flavored jelly beans): the actively managed fund. Unlike conventional

ETFs, the actively managed fund doesn't seek to mimic the performance of a particular index.

But What About Costs and Transparency?

The step into active management seems the last frontier of the ETF
world. Scott Stark, founder of Stark Strategic Capital Management, believes that these ETFs are the next logical step, but he urges investors
to be cautious: "If the costs are too high, it could be one of those crazes
that hits the market and eventually falls off the radar screen."

One of the major obstacles actively managed ETFs face is providing the typical transparency of standard ETFs while offering accurate
up-to-the-minute pricing throughout the trading day. A major advantage and primary selling point of most ETFs is their built-in transparency. Knowing what's in the underlying index means that you know
what you're holding. With actively managed ETFs, however, the
fund's manager can opt to buy or sell a stock at any time.

Active management means holdings are actively bought and sold,
traded in and out. But what if it gets a little too active? What if the
fund's manager is in there, trading stocks as they rise and fall, racking
up fees and cutting into profits? Managers have to be careful—too
much movement could just lead to higher costs and less tax efficiency.
At that point, you would have to seriously question whether the actively managed ETF is even worth it. It doesn't seem that this question can be honestly answered until these ETFs are released into the
market and the marketplace can see how they perform in real life.

What's in Store?

One of the actively managed ETFs in the pipeline is the Current
Yield fund (YYY) from Bear Stearns. This fund invests in money mar-
ket/short-term fixed-income obligations, corporate debt, asset-backed

securities, municipal bonds, and other products. The fund's manager, Scott Pavlak, says he uses a top-down approach for sector allocation combined with extensive research on individual securities. No sector will make up more than 25 percent of the funds, and no single security will be weighted more than 5 percent.

Vanguard's actively managed ETF is another share class of the Vanguard Inflation Protected Securities fund. This fund seeks to provide investors with inflation protection and income consistent with investment in inflation-indexed securities. This strategy has been successful and is considered to be an easy way to keep costs from spiraling out of control.

The entry of Vanguard in the race to launch the first actively managed ETF was a bit of a surprise because Bogle has been such a vocal critic of ETFs. However, it makes more sense when you realize that his successor, John Brennan, has embraced ETFs as another way to distribute mutual funds. Vanguard is now the third largest ETF firm in the business, with more than 33 offerings and $31 billion in assets as of late 2007. The Vanguard actively managed ETF is not as much of a head scratcher as you might suppose.

iMyth: Active ETFs Will Be Just Like Mutual Funds

Actively managed ETFs sound a lot like plain old mutual funds, but there are a few differences. You might have better shareholder protection—all assets that go into or out of an ETF are at net asset value. Mutual funds don't have many safety mechanisms in place to protect the shareholders against active trading, which drives up the cost for everyone. Could actively managed ETFs be a death knell for mutual funds? For most individual investors, says fund manager Gary Gastineau, ETFs contain a better structure than a conventional mutual fund. Gastineau believes there's no question that, once launched, actively managed ETFs will ultimately be more attractive than mutual funds. We're reserving judgment until we see them. If they can duplicate the transparency, low costs, and flexibility of their indexed sisters, they will be worth a closer look.

Active Management vs. Mutual Funds

Not everyone is in favor of active management. The SEC solicited public comment about actively managed ETFs, and the Investment Company Institute responded to the call. The institute cited three areas of particular concern in its letter: transparency and how holdings would be disclosed, the implications of adding an actively managed ETF to a traditional mutual fund, and the potential for other conflicts of interest.

In its letter, the institute expressed its biggest concern, the most far-reaching issue being a portfolio's transparency and how lack of transparency hurts investors. Remember, the secrecy of mutual funds is a major reason ETFs became so popular in the first place. Will investors view active management as a giant step backward? An actively managed ETF might be unable to maintain a market value tracking NAV, as traditional ETFs do, because the real-time holdings would not be known. And if the real-time holdings *do* become known, costs will be associated with putting out that information.

At the very least, the institute suggested that such "opaque" funds be required to let investors know just what they're getting into with clear disclosure highlighting risks.

The SEC is in no hurry to approve applications for actively managed ETFs. The SEC has been reviewing the matter for years now, and in previous releases on the matter, it has questioned whether actively managed ETFs will give investors the information needed to ensure that the markets are still liquid for ETF shares. If the holdings information isn't updated as frequently as it is with traditional ETFs, investors might not be as willing to create or redeem ETF shares, which could lead to ETFs trading at wider bid/ask spreads and bigger discounts or premiums against their NAVs.

The biggest hang-up facing active ETFs is management itself. Most managers don't want to disclose their holdings more than once per quarter, as currently required by the SEC. Letting investors in on the movements of a fund has two drawbacks: It can enable some traders to monitor the fund and then ride its coattails. It also allows traders to see if a fund is heading in a particular direction, and then swoop in and try to beat the fund. This forces managers to trade at higher prices or to sell at lower prices, hurting overall fund performance. We can't imagine that many of them would be too excited to offer both transparency *and* active management.

Vanguard is seeking to put these concerns to rest by pointing out that the Inflation-Protected Securities Fund is not a fancy one—it keeps almost all of its money in highly liquid U.S. Treasuries, whose principal values are adjusted for changes in the Consumer Price Index (CPI). It usually holds only about 20 securities.

It all really boils down to one thing: we can speculate until the end of time, but most of our questions and concerns won't be answered until investors and analysts can see just how actively managed ETFs behave in the real world.

ETF of ETFs: The Latest Package

Imitating the hedge fund world, in late 2007 (as of this writing), the PowerShares Capital group registered to offer a fund investing in other ETFs. Instead of holding one fixed portfolio, the new fund simply holds other ETFs. Bruce Bond, a marketing executive with PowerShares, said the new fund is a "core" holding, allowing investors to also hold "satellite" ETFs in other areas.

Of course, as with the hedge fund products with a similar strategy, a packager of the ETFs imposes an extra layer of fees—in this case, an extra .25 percent annually. In addition to reduced returns due to the higher expenses, investors might be subject to manager risk. This largely depends on which funds are picked and how well they perform. It would be wise to wait on this new product until some performance numbers are posted.

The Evolution Continues

When you look at how far ETFs have come in such a short period of time, you can't help but wonder where this is all going. Almost every step of the way, ETFs have continued to shock, surprise, and delight investors. When they first arrived on the scene in 1993, few people could have conceived that they would one day be serious challengers to the mutual fund throne. As providers continue to offer new ETFs, naysayers have been proven wrong again and again.

Today ETFs are where mutual funds were 30 years ago. They're still relatively small in number and going head-to-head with what has been America's favorite investment tool for decades. Critics of their rapid proliferation speak out against them. Many of these same doubts surfaced when mutual funds were at this level in their evolution. In the not-too-distant past, people wondered if there were too many mutual funds, if they were growing too quickly, and if there *wasn't* a sector for which there was a mutual fund. Industry critics wondered, isn't it all just getting a little out of hand?

Claims that currency ETFs could never work were proved wrong. Critics said commodity ETFs weren't going to take off, but investors have been clamoring to hop on board a sector that had long been denied to them. Now there's a battle over whether ETFs can be incorporated into 401(k) plans, but Invest n Retire's Darwin Abrahamson's software has shown that to be wrong.

It's clear: All of those things *could* work and are working. Now it's time for analysts and investors to start thinking about what's coming next and where this is all headed instead of shooting down various types of ETFs as unworkable. The one thing we do know for sure is that they're a huge hit and they're here to stay. The sky is the limit! It's up to investors and analysts to sort out how high it will all go.

The consensus seems to be positive overall. And by that, we mean ETFs won't be dead in two decades.

In fact, it's a good sign for ETFs that their biggest detractors are even getting in the game. The old establishment names of Vanguard and Fidelity have entered the business.

The "Height of Esoterica"?

Are ETFs going too fast and furious for their own good? According to Fierce Finance, at the 7th Annual World Series of ETFs, a few investors began to gripe that the various permutations of hyperfocused ETFs are the "height of esoterica." They also said that they were slowly chipping away at the appeal that ETFs initially had of being simple, basic vehicles in which people could invest with little muss or fuss. Specialized ETFs are muddying the waters, usually unnecessarily, these investors said. Are they really needed?

We take the stand that these things *are* necessary. Having a wide range of available ETF products only fosters more competition, and nothing benefits the consumer more than a little bit of good, old-fashioned competition. It's good for the spirit. We also say, give investors a little credit. They aren't children who should be allowed to use only the dull-edged scissors. So many things out there can get them into trouble that worrying about ETFs doesn't do anyone any good.

ETFs aren't going to overtake mutual funds anytime soon. That's not because of any failure on their part—it's just that mutual funds are a Goliath to ETF's David. In 2007, assets in mutual funds based in the United States were at $12.3 trillion. Contrast that with the $688 billion in ETF assets, and you can see that ETFs have a long way to go. But bear in mind that it took ETFs a mere 14 years to get to a place that mutual funds took 56 years to get to, so wherever "there" is, ETFs are getting to that point at a fast pace. It's remarkable when you think about it. Everything is happening faster in the Internet age, and word spreads quickly when something new comes along, especially a good deal.

All signs are pointing to a positive and exciting future. Nearly every day, new ETFs are being introduced. Providers spring up, offering ETFs to cover previously unseen and unheard-of asset classes and sectors. In the future, we'll likely have new ETF providers offering their products in those same sectors, but with differently constructed indexes.

iMoney Strategy: The Bottom Line

If you're drawn to new ETF products, educate yourself before you invest. Investing in ETFs demands that you become more informed, especially as products tend to get more specialized and focused. We think that the near future of ETFs will involve more soul-searching. Ask yourself whether it's really necessary to have a cancer ETF, or whether it's beneficial to follow gold or currency futures. After all, you can have too many investment options. Who knows? You might decide that some of the new ETFs are both necessary and beneficial. It's still important, however, to see where they fit into your portfolio and stomach for risk. Will they add value or diversification? Are they filling a gap such as hedging against inflation or U.S. stock-market declines? If so, can they do it efficiently and in a manner that reduces overall portfolio risk? In the end, any ETF that you consider adding should do something that you haven't already done. If it's not the missing piece to your portfolio puzzle, you might not need it. But for those portfolio puzzles with missing pieces, ETFs are most likely to be just what you need.

12

iMoney ETF Portfolios

I started with ETFs because it was an easy, low-cost, and low-risk way to invest for someone with minimal starting capital. My goals for the future are to save as much as possible so that I can have enough money for a down payment on a home by the time I am 24. (I am currently 21).

—ETF Trends reader Dylan Curtis

Most of us can remember the euphoria of the stock market in the late 1990s. It was hard to avoid talking about the way things were going. It was easy; no matter who you were or what you bought, you made money.

It was a great time to be a money manager, Tom says. His clients were happy and loved talking about their portfolios. People who weren't investing were looking for managers to help get them into the stock market so they could participate in the boom and not feel left out of the conversation at cocktail parties and on the golf course. It was the best of times.

Tom has a friend who decided it was better to be a day trader than to sell real estate. Another guy he plays tennis with couldn't help but talk about the stocks he was buying every time we got on the court. If your cab driver found out that you were in the investment business, he would give you his stock tips. A few cabbies had their computers in their cars and picked stocks while waiting for their next fare.

The downside was that you knew it was going to end at some point. Saying things like, "We have to grab this while we can 'cause it isn't going to last forever" was popular. A few clients wondered why their portfolios weren't up as much as the NASDAQ 100, suggesting we might be too conservatively invested. You remember those times. For many, it was a great learning experience.

The Rules Everyone Should Follow

Before you do anything else, there's a basic strategy everyone should follow. It doesn't matter who you are or what your goals are or how much money you have—these strategies are the same across the board. The goals investors have often vary from person to person, but it can safely be said that everyone has one thing in common: They don't want to outlive their money. This is why strategy matters and why you should choose your plan of attack and stick by it. Here are some key guidelines:

- **Buy and hold.** This is one of the most common strategies you'll come across, and it works for most investors. It involves just that—buying and holding. If you choose this strategy, you should pay no mind to market swings on any given day. Your eyes are on the prize, and the prize is way in the future. You believe that, over time, the markets will go up. If you sit back and do nothing, regardless of how your portfolio holdings shift, then you are practicing a pure buy-and-hold strategy. Why go for the buy and hold? Warren Buffett is among many successful investors who favor the strategy. It costs less, and there are tax benefits involved because the IRS taxes long-term capital gains at a lower rate than short-term ones. You also won't be trading as much, which means fewer commissions and other fees.

- **Rebalance.** The only changes, if any, to your buy-and-hold portfolio over time will generally be to rebalance. For example, if the stocks in your portfolio rise so much in value that they increase from 40 percent of the portfolio to 70 percent, you might do some moving around to bring everything back into proportion by selling some of the stocks or purchasing securities in other asset classes. This is known as active investing or tactical asset allocation.

- **Ignore the noise.** If you can tune out the random static the market generates every day, you believe in Princeton economics professor Burton Malkiel's theory of the Random Walk, which basically says that the prices of securities are random and uninfluenced by anything that has happened in the past. For this reason, attempting to outperform the market is a fruitless task, so you might as well just sit still. Don't believe the hype. Ignore ads and testimonials that claim the potential for large profits from active trading. Those ads should have a "results not typical" disclaimer because the truth is that the profits could be few or nil, and it could all happen in the blink of an eye.

- **Remember that it's not *when* you buy, but *what* you buy.** According to a 1986 study by Brinson, Hood, and Beebower, 95 percent of the time it's not *when* you buy or sell, but *what* you buy or sell. Asset allocation decides how your portfolio will do over the long haul. Carl Delfeld, president of Chartwell Partners, suggests you take a different tack and divvy up your portfolio instead of dividing it up into various things, risking all of your assets. For example, have one portfolio for growth and one for core. The core portfolio is for the safer, low-risk investments and is the larger of the two. The growth portfolio is for the high-risk stuff: currencies, health care, high-tech, and emerging markets. Having two portfolios with different objectives will ensure that if you lose your shirt in one area, at least your entire portfolio won't go down with it.

- **If you want to be more active, have a discipline and stick to it.** What if the buy-and-hold strategy is too tame for you? You crave action. You're itching to monitor the markets first thing in the morning until last thing in the afternoon. You want to make trades. You want to buy new ETFs. You want to be your own active manager? And why would you want to do that? Here are a few reasons: if you take an active role, you think you'll be able to enhance your role even more over time. You might even be able to sleep better at night. You like trading. Some people love it. It's important to figure out why you're not in the buy-and-hold category of investor, if you're really looking to take charge of your portfolio. You need to be honest with yourself and be willing to put in the time and effort to get results. You need to do it because it gets your blood pumping. You *live* for this stuff. If you can't say that, then perhaps you should reconsider your motives and determine whether this is right for you. To be an active trader, you need to have a thorough knowledge of the securities markets, along with disciplined trading techniques. After all, you're going to be going head-to-head with professionals who do this for a living. They're well trained and they know what they're doing. You'll quickly be in over your head if you try to roll with them before you're ready.

- **Ask yourself whether you're a Nervous Nellie.** If you don't have a lot of money to spare, you're new to investing, or you just can't afford to lose anything, don't take any chances. Imagine losing some of your funds. Can you stomach that thought? If not, active trading is *not* right for you.

- **Always consider the costs.** Not only could you lose your initial investment, but you also can't forget about the commissions. You'll be paying something on each trade you make, and it will quickly add up. Does it sound like we're trying to scare you? Well, we are, because active trading isn't a game. It's serious business, and if you can read through all the caveats without your stomach flipping or breaking into a cold sweat, then you just might have the nerve to do it.

Do You Track Trends?

Somewhere between the buy-and-hold strategy and active trading is trend following. It's the strategy Tom recommends for his clients and the basis of much discussion on ETF Trends—watching for trends and setting stop losses to minimize the damage. Most important, we stick to our plan regardless of what happens. In the book *Trend Following*, author Michael Covel says that the objective is to have a clearly defined strategy. Covel pokes holes in the argument that the analysis and projections of Wall Street are the end-all and be-all of investing, and says instead that they're actually of very limited use to investors. His theory is that you can do best when you're in tune with a trend, and we subscribe to his way of thinking.

Getting in tune is simple, and getting there involves adhering to a strict discipline. It means ignoring your intuition and your gut and instead following only what is right there in front of you. There's no anticipation of something going one way or the other. The only time you take action is when something is actually occurring.

Tom's firm's investment strategy uses the 200-day moving average as the basis for all of its decisions. If the price drops below the long-term trend line or dips to 8 percent off its recent highs, it's time to sell. It's time to get back in when things begin to show signs of a turnaround. When something is sold, the firm views the cash generated as a "free agent," meaning that it is free to be used for any investment for which a trend is developing. If no areas show an up trend or momentum at that time, the money stays in a money market fund.

When you can't be in a winning position, the least you can do is minimize the hit your portfolio takes. You never know if it's a tiny, fixable leak or a sinking ship when the numbers tumble, and that's why it's best to bail out when you can—before you wind up dog-paddling in the middle of the ocean. Having a stop loss is just another way of saying, don't get sucked into the hype. Don't let the excitement that analysts and friends might feel about a particular stock sway you or keep you from making smart choices with your money. Be wise, and don't get caught up in a giant wave of possibly undeserved enthusiasm about a particular fund, or you could just wind up with a mouthful of seaweed.

What do you do when things turn around? That means you'll need an entry strategy, too. When something is sold, it's helpful to look at the cash generated as a "free agent," whether it's in an asset class, a global region, or a market sector. If none of those areas is showing any particular momentum, hang on to the money in a money market fund until something turns around.

What's a trend? A general rule is that if something has been happening in the markets for 20 uninterrupted days, you've got yourself a trend. Anything can cause the market to take a big spike up or a plummeting descent down on a particular day, and that in and of itself isn't the most troubling scenario. But if the numbers are heading lower and lower for a stretch of time, you've got a situation. History has already shown us, for example, that the Dow Jones Industrial Average moves in well-defined cycles. Over the last 110 years, there have been four bull markets and four bear markets. The stock market typically enters long periods of high returns, followed by long periods of lower ones.

How do you know when a bear is a bear and when a bull is a bull? In a *bull market*, each successive high point is even higher than the one that came before it (higher highs offset by higher lows). The opposite occurs in a *bear market*—the trend drops and offsetting price levels do not rise above the previous high (lower lows offset by lower highs). Long-term trends actually stick around much longer than most investors realize. Think about it—how many times have you heard the financial pundits sound the alarm after a bad week in the markets? But a trend's establishment is never that simple. You don't trade based on long-term trends alone. It's more advisable to use them for guidance. For example, if the trend is up, the probability is that the odds will favor long trades and investments over short ones.

Basing decisions on probabilities doesn't always work, but if you invest using them, over time you should be able to do well. If every day you calculate the general trend of a market, through either ETFs or a particular global region, why not simply allocate to those markets riding above their trend lines and steer clear of the ones that have fallen below? It's simple:

1. Allocate your assets to those areas that are above their trend lines.

2. Sell whatever positions fall below those trend lines or those that dip 8 percent off their highs, whatever comes first.

A Brief History of the Moving Average Strategy

When Tom worked at Fidelity, two of his clients were Dick and Doug Fabian. Dick was a transplanted New Yorker who arrived in Southern California around the same time the Dodgers did. During 1973 and 1974, the S&P declined 45 percent. Dick was a financial advisor at the time, and his clients suffered along with most Americans. He made a commitment to himself, his family, and his clients to try to avoid ever reliving that experience.

Dick spent weeks in the basement of the Long Beach State Library, researching markets, trends, and technical analysis, and concluded that the general trends of the market can be identified mathematically. His 39-week average indicator was the key trading indicator. He launched a newsletter in 1976 called *Telephone Switch Newsletter*. This was shortly after mutual fund companies allowed investors to switch within fund families, from a growth fund to a money market or vice versa. The *Telephone Switch Newsletter* grew into one of the most popular mutual fund investment newsletters in the country during the 1980s and early 1990s.

Dick always said there was a higher probability that investors would follow a plan if it was simple, and following a 39-week average over the decades has helped investors avoid bear markets and participate in bull markets. Today many active investors are comfortable identifying a 200-day moving average, a well-known indicator for identifying general trends in the marketplace.

When the S&P 500 goes below its 200-day moving average, it will be talked about on CNBC and throughout the financial press as an indicator that there's weakness in the markets. That same 200-day moving average can be applied to all asset classes, sectors, and global regions. The key is having the discipline to monitor the average and sticking to it consistently. Better yet, if you are an active trader, you have available a number of new ETF hedging tools.

Going Your Own Way: Using the 200-Day Moving Average

Whatever strategy you choose, the most important thing is this: Be disciplined, have an exit strategy, and set stop losses. If you say you're going to do X when Y happens, and Y *does* happen, follow through. Don't rationalize or get emotionally attached to your holdings.

Even if you've invested in a scrappy little company that has done well before it falls on hard times, don't talk yourself out of following through with what you always said you would do just because you like the company. It's not personal—it's business, right? On the flip side of that, if you plan to hold for the long-term and your investments suddenly take a big spill, stick to the plan. Don't suddenly fret, worry, and sell everything.

As you manage your portfolio, you might feel a need to always have a set amount of money designated for a certain area, whether it's India or large-caps or something else. In this case, hang on to the cash until that area moves above its 200-day moving average or gains 5 percent from its recent low. No matter what your plan is when it comes to investing or what your ultimate goals might be, do your best to keep your poker face at all times. When emotions enter the equation, it becomes nearly impossible to remain rational or objective.

Spread It Around: Asset Allocation

It doesn't matter what kind of investor you are: you need to diversify. Consider this: If your portfolio is invested almost exclusively in European ETFs, you'd be up a creek if European corporations in those ETFs took a sudden nosedive. Giving one sector that kind of emphasis can knock you out for the count. Asset allocation helps you keep your major risks low by spreading them out over a series of smaller risks.

Many investors don't do so well with asset allocation, unfortunately. Just as some couples go into a marriage without sorting out the key issues *before* the rings are exchanged ("What? You want to adopt a dozen Malawian children?!"), some investors put their money in this and that, chasing trends and getting caught up in a never-ending stream of hype without giving serious thought to what their ultimate goals are or whether they might have too much money in a particular area. Here are some things to remember:

- **Time horizon.** This is the expected number of months, years, or decades you will be investing to achieve a particular goal. The longer the time horizon, the more time you have to recover from downturns in the market. On the other hand, if you're saving up for something a few years down the road, it's unlikely you'd want to take a big gamble. And if you're relatively close to retirement, don't put most of your money in the stock market.

- **Risk tolerance.** This is your comfort level with losing some or all of your original investment, the tradeoff being that the potential returns are greater. You could be 25 years old and still remain uncomfortable with the idea of investing everything you have in something risky. It never changes, however, that the greater the risk, the greater the potential reward or the more spectacular the fall. How comfortable are you knowing that you could lose money? How much of a loss would you be able to stomach? Follow Warren Buffet's two basic rules: "Number one, don't lose money. Number two, don't forget rule number one."

When you've figured out your time horizon and your risk tolerance, you're ready to move forward and start breaking it down. We can't tell you what your acceptable level of risk is—that is completely up to you, no matter what your age. Some experts advise a riskier portfolio when you're younger, becoming gradually more conservative as you approach retirement. But if *you* aren't comfortable with a particular level of risk, that's enough reason for you not to take it on. You know how they tell you to stop using the treadmill if you feel faint or dizzy? The same thing goes when investing.

Determining your risk tolerance is the most important thing you can do before you invest. Financial institutions have "risk calculators" online to help you determine your comfort level by asking you a series of questions. Answer honestly, and you should get a good result. Enter "investment risk calculator" into the search engine of your choice, and you should get plenty of results to help you.

Don't Want to Do It Yourself? Find a Fiduciary

Some financial experts believe that asset allocation is the single most important decision you'll ever make with your investments—many even believe that it's more important than the actual investments you make. Daunting, isn't it?

Two levels of diversification exist: between asset classes and within asset classes. It's important that you pinpoint which segments of your asset categories perform differently, depending on the winds of the market. One way to diversify within an asset class is to invest in a wide range of companies or sectors. This is one major reason ETFs are so appealing. They follow an index and already offer built-in diversification with lower risk than what would come with buying individual stocks. Some experts have already done the legwork for you, making it much easier than individual investments.

As with anything else, it's important not to lose sight of your long-term strategies. Keep in mind that just because you can invest through ETFs, doesn't mean you should. The good news is that you don't have to do it all yourself. You can find several possible portfolios in the following pages, on Internet sites, or by hiring a professional to put together a customized allocation plan.

If you choose to work with an advisor, here's one piece of advice: don't work with a commissioned salesperson whose only interest is selling you a raft of products. Choose a registered investment advisor or fee-only financial planner who acts as a *fiduciary*. A fiduciary takes legal responsibility for his recommendations. Unlike salespeople, who will make you sign an agreement that forces you to use their industry arbitration forum in the event of a dispute, a fiduciary can be sued. You can also check a person's background at www.finra.org/investorinformation/investorprotection/p005882. Be sure to review the advisory disclosure forms for any registered investment advisor you choose. A fiduciary's ADV forms, filed with the SEC, must be updated annually. Look carefully at Form ADV, Part II, Schedule F, which details all potential conflicts of interest.

iMyth: Once I Have My Portfolio, There's No \Need to Change It

Sure, you can sit back, relax, and enjoy the show, but just as asset allocation isn't a one-size-fits-all venture, it's not a do-it-once-and-forget-about-it venture, either. Over time, as the markets change and as your financial goals change, you must consider whether reallocation is right for you. The most common reason investors change their asset allocation is that they've moved into a new stage of life; typically that means they're just closer to retirement age and are interested in decreasing their risk further. Smart investors don't mess around with their asset allocations just because a particular sector or asset class isn't performing well relative to another. Instead, they *rebalance,* which just means bringing a portfolio back to its original asset allocation breakdown. The primary reason for rebalancing is to ensure that the portfolio isn't overconcentrated in one area or asset class. For example, say that you've decided that your bond investments will be 20 percent of your portfolio, but because of recent changes, they're now somehow 30 percent. You need to either sell some bonds or invest in another underweighted category to get back to your original allocation. Rebalancing isn't without its controversies, though. Mutual fund manager Peter Brown has referred to the practice as "cutting the flowers and watering the weeds." It's a colorful analogy, if not good advice.

Finding a Model Portfolio for You

Investors are almost like snowflakes—oh, we're sure that here and there are two that happen to be exactly alike, but for the most part, they're unique. They have unique goals, unique portfolios, unique risk profiles, and unique interests. No one can tell an investor exactly what to do because it simply depends on so many factors: where you are in life, how old you are, how much you are able to invest, what your personal interests might be.

Diversifying with ETFs becomes a little more of a challenge when they are whittled down into narrow sectors. That's when you need to exercise caution and do intensive research to make sure you aren't overweighted in one area or allowing any big gaps in another. When you're presented with an array of asset classes and ever-specialized sectors, the temptation is to just go nuts and grab hold of everything you can fit into your pockets without considering the overall portfolio.

Only you can decide what your needs are, and this section offers some ideas to help you decide how to meet them through investing. If you've done your homework on how much risk you can tolerate and have a good idea of how you'd like to proceed, the following are some sample portfolios to get you started. They are largely designed to match your investment personality and your time of life.

Feel free to mix and match if you'd like to incorporate some elements of one portfolio into another. These are merely suggestions. If you have more focused goals or needs, you might want to hire a fee-only financial planner or registered investor advisor (see the previous section) to set up a customized portfolio.

Model Portfolios

The Go-Getter (Aggressive)

Who are you? You're a young 20-something. You've just entered the workforce, perhaps in your chosen field of study, and now you're in it for the long haul. You've got lots of time to prepare for retirement and you don't need the money right now, so you're prepared to stomach a considerable amount of risk if it means being comfortable in 40 years. You want to maximize return and, therefore, be as aggressive as you can possibly be.

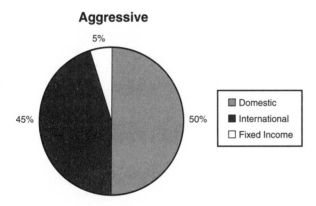

Aggressive

5%

45%   50%

Domestic
International
Fixed Income

Figure 12.1

Table 12.1   Holdings for the Aggressive Investor

SPDRs	SPY	10%
Vanguard Mid-Cap	VO	15%
iShares Russell 2000 Index	IWM	15%
PowerShares QQQ	QQQQ	10%
iShares MSCI EAFE Index	EFA	20%
iShares MSCI Emerging Markets Index	EEM	10%
Claymore/BNY BRIC	EEB	5%
iShares S&P Latin America 40 Index	ILF	10%
iShares Lehman 20+ Year Treasury	TLT	5%
		100%

The Whoa, Slow Down a Little (Moderately Aggressive)

Who are you? You're in your late 20s or early 30s. Maybe you're about ready to think about starting a family and buying a home, and you're thinking about the future a little more. You're still in it for the long term and you still want to continue the good growth of your portfolio. For that reason, you'll stay more on the aggressive side of things and the volatility will remain, but you're ready to scale back ever so slightly.

Moderately Aggressive

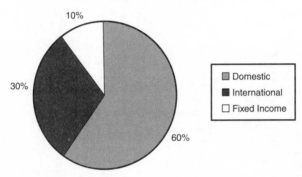

Figure 12.2

Table 12.2 Holdings for the Moderately Aggressive Investor

SPDRs	SPY	20%
Vanguard Mid-Cap	VO	15%
iShares Russell 2000 Index	IWM	15%
Rydex S&P Equal Weight	RSP	10%
iShares MSCI EAFE Index	EFA	10%
iShares MSCI Emerging Markets Index	EEM	10%
Claymore/BNY BRIC	EEB	5%
iShares S&P Latin America 40 Index	ILF	5%
iShares Lehman 20+ Year Treasury	TLT	10%
		100%

The In-Betweener (Moderate)

Who are you? Now you're in the thick of it. You own a home, you're mid-career, you've got a family to support. You've still got a ways to go until retirement, but it's sure looming a lot closer than it was when you graduated college. It's no longer a day way off in the distant future—it's getting closer all the time. You need to think about balance. You still want that growth, but you also want to protect what you've built so far because starting over at this point wouldn't be good.

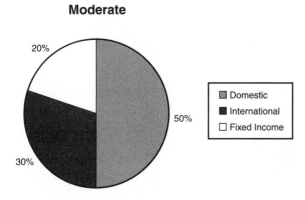

Figure 12.3

Table 12.3   Holdings for the Moderate Investor

SPDRs	SPY	30%
Vanguard Mid-Cap	VO	10%
iShares Russell 2000 Index	IWM	10%
iShares MSCI EAFE Index	EFA	15%
iShares MSCI Emerging Markets Index	EEM	15%
iShares Lehman 20+ Year Treasury	TLT	10%
iShares Lehman 1–3 Year Treasury	SHY	10%
		100%

The Almost There (Moderately Conservative)

Who are you? You're pretty close to retirement, and maybe you've even got kids headed to college. Your house might be close to be paid off and you're gearing up for some pretty sweet Golden Years. You need a little bit of income to make up the difference and fill in a few gaps here and there, but you also want to maintain a little bit of growth while adding stability to your portfolio—you're not quite at the finish line yet.

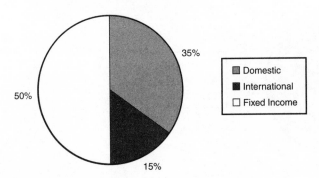

Moderately Conservative

35%

■ Domestic
■ International
□ Fixed Income

50%

15%

Figure 12.4

Table 12.4   Holdings for the Moderately Conservative Investor

SPDRs	SPY	15%
Rydex S&P Equal Weight	RSP	15%
iShares Russell 2000 Index	IWM	5%
iShares MSCI EAFE Index	EFA	10%
iShares MSCI Emerging Markets Index	EEM	5%
iShares Lehman 20+ Year Treasury	TLT	15%
iShares Lehman 1–3 Year Treasury	SHY	15%
iShares Lehman 7–10 Year Treasury	IEF	15%
iShares Lehman TIPS Bond	TIP	5%
		100%

The I'm Outta Here (Conservative)

Who are you? You're free, that's what! You're at the finish line. Retired. Finito. Let the fun begin! If you've invested wisely throughout the years, gradually making your portfolio more conservative, you should have a nice amount of money to get you through. You can spoil your grandkids, surprise your spouse with a trip to Europe, or just take it easy and enjoy the simple things. Now your portfolio is aimed at getting some income—growth is no longer the big concern here.

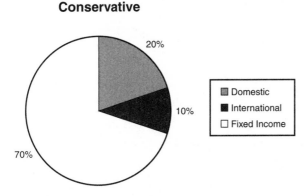

Figure 12.5

Table 12.5   Holdings for the Conservative Investor

SPDRs	SPY	10%
Rydex S&P Equal Weight	RSP	10%
iShares MSCI EAFE Index	EFA	10%
iShares Lehman 20+ Year Treasury	TLT	10%
iShares Lehman 1–3 Year Treasury	SHY	20%
iShares Lehman 7–10 Year Treasury	IEF	20%
iShares Lehman TIPS Bond	TIP	20%
		100%

Too Much of a Good Thing

Remember John Steinbeck's *Of Mice and Men*? The dim Lenny would accidentally kill whatever he loved because he didn't know his own strength and wound up getting a little too rough. Well, it's possible to kill your portfolio by getting too rough, too. By overdiversifying, you could be biting off more than you can chew. Do you have the kind of time and energy to devote to keeping track of a large number of companies?

Overdiversifying involves other problems, too:

- Your standards will slacken. If you're taking on whatever comes along, how selective can you really be? You might even be okay with taking on greater risk because you're not putting as much into one specific company. Sharp declines aren't going to stick out as much, meaning they might slip right by you.

- Your individual investments won't have the same punch they did before. Your capital could be spread so far and wide that even the best investment you ever made will have only a tiny bit of impact on your portfolio. The moral is, don't overindulge. Moderation is a good strategy for dieting *and* stock picking.

When it comes to ETFs, the bad news is that you are your own worst enemy. The good news is that you're your own worst enemy. That means *you*, and only you, control how well you do (well, within reason).

iMoney Strategy: Staying the Course: Becoming and Remaining Disciplined

If you keep in mind the words of Burton Malkiel that "you must distinguish between your attitude *toward* and your capacity *for* risk," you should be okay in the ETF arena. After all, who's a better judge of how much risk you can take? Unless you're retiring soon, time could be on your side. Stocks have returned about 10 percent per year since 1926 and the power of compounding doubles your money in about seven years. But to achieve that performance, you need to stay invested in your plan.

When you know where you're going, stay the course. It's like a diet. You've heard people complain, or perhaps even you've complained, "I don't know what I'm doing wrong! No matter what I do, I *can't lose weight!*" It turns out that you've been sneaking down to the kitchen for a midnight snack, or you went to the gym only once this week. The reason you haven't lost is that you haven't been sticking to the diet. It's the same with investing. Want your portfolio to flourish? Stick to the plan.

References

Introduction

The single best source on the mutual fund industry is its trade association, The Investment Company Institute (www.ici.org), which provided several background statistics for this section.

Chapter 1

Much of the Bogle research mother lode is contained in his books on mutual funds. The figures quoted in this section are from his presentations and his latest work, *The Little Book of Common Sense Investing* (Wiley, 2007), which distills most of Bogle's findings. John has also interviewed Bogle several times over the past decade. Also, check out the Bogle Financial Research Center at www.vanguard.com/bogle_site/bogle_home.html.

For current risk-adjusted returns on ETFs, see www.morningstar.com, or consult its primer *ETFs 150* (Wiley, 2007), which profiles the top ETFs.

The issue of tracking error was discussed in "Analyzing International ETFs: A Challenge," by David Hoffman, *Investment News*, November 19, 2007.

Chapter 2

All Financial Matters. *What Is Fundamental Indexing?* 2006. http://allfinancialmatters.com/2006/11/14/what-is-fundamental-indexing/.

Arnott, Rob. *Rob Arnott Discusses the Fundamental Approach to Stock Market Indexing.* Pimco Bonds, 2005. www.pimco.com/leftnav/product+focus/2005/arnott+fundamental+indexing+interview.htm.

Bailyn, Russell. *Indexes: What You Should Know.* Russell Bailyn's Financial Planning Blog, 2007. www.russellbailyn.com/weblog/2007/04/indexes_what_you_should_know.html.

Befumo, Randy, and Schay, Alex. *History of the Dow.* The Motley Fool. www.fool.com/ddow/historyofthedow5.htm.

CFTech. *Dow Jones Averages Chronology.* 1884–1995.

Dogs of the Dow. *Dow History.* www.dogsofthedow.com/dowhist.htm.

Investopedia. *Computing the PEG Ratio and Determining a Company's Earnings Growth.* www.investopedia.com/ask/answers/06/pegratioearningsgrowthrate.asp.

Little, Ken. *Understanding Price to Earnings Ratio.* About.com. http://stocks.about.com/od/evaluatingstocks/a/pe.htm.

Middleton, Timothy. *Buy the S&P 500 with Better Returns.* MSN Money, 2004. http://moneycentral.msn.com/content/p100259.asp.

The Motley Fool. *Motley Fool Index Center.* www.fool.com/school/indices/sp500.htm

Spence, John. *Tempest in an Index Fund: Robert Arnott and John Bogle Clash over Best Indexing Strategy.* MarketWatch, 2007. www.marketwatch.com/news/story/rivals-arnott-bogle-spar-over/story.aspx?guid=%7BDAFCCB14-21EA-44E0-B919-A2D484544413%7D.

Standard & Poor's. *S&P 500 Description.* www2.standardandpoors.com.

Vanguard. *Vanguard 500 Index Fund Investor Shares.* https://personal.vanguard.com.

Wikipedia. *Fundamentally Based Indexes.* http://en.wikipedia.org/wiki/fundamental_weighting.

Bogle's work is again referenced from his presentation materials mentioned in Chapter 1.

John Wasik has conducted numerous interviews with Robert Arnott over the past several years and featured his work in his Bloomberg News columns. More information is available at www.researchaffiliates.com. For a classic text on value investing, refer to *The Intelligent Investor*, by Benjamin Graham (Harper, 1973), with a Foreword by Warren Buffett.

For an informative study on broker-managed index funds, see the Zero Alpha Group report "Huge Broker Penalty Sees Unwary Index Fund Investors Paying 3 Times More in Fund Expenses" at www.zeroalphagroup.com.

The classic Morningstar study on closet indexing was cited in the *New York Times* piece "The Index Monster in Your Closet" by Richard A. Oppel, Jr. (October 10, 1999).

Chapter 3

AXA Financial Protection. *Growth vs. Value: Two Approaches to Stock Selection*. www.axaonline.com/rs/3p/sp/5040.html.

Barker, Bill. *70 Times Better Than the Next Microsoft*. The Motley Fool, 2006. www.fool.com/investing/small-cap/2006/01/12/70-times-better-than-the-next-microsoft.aspx.

Befumo, Randy. *A Lesson in Tax Efficiency*. The Motley Fool. www.fool.com/school/mutualfunds/costs/efficiency.htm.

Custodio, Tony. *How Large Are Large-Cap Stocks?* 401Kafe. www.infoplease.com/finance/tips/money/moneyman_101199.html.

Elfenbein, Eddy. *Accessing Micro-Caps via ETFs*. Seeking Alpha, 2005. http://seekingalpha.com/article/4440-accessing-micro-caps-via-etfs-etfs-iwc-fdm-pzi.

Ellentuck, Albert B. *Investing in Tax Efficient Funds*. All Business. www.allbusiness.com/personal-finance/investing/255356-1.html.

ETF Guide. *History of Exchange Traded Funds*. www.etfguide.com/exchangetradedfunds.htm.

ETF Zone. *ETF Liquidity Myth Dispelled*. http://finance.yahoo.com/etf/education/05.

Funds 400 Investing Classroom. *Mid-Cap Stocks: What They Are*. http://news.morningstar.com/classroom2/course.asp?docId=2996&page=2&CN=com&t1=1192487808.

Greenwald, Igor. *In Battle of Growth vs. Value, Value Wins*. Smart Money, 2007. www.smartmoney.com/invisiblehand/index.cfm?story=20070717.

Investopedia. *Definition of Small Cap*. www.investopedia.com/terms/s/small-cap.asp.

Investopedia. *Introduction to Small Caps*. www.investopedia.com/articles/01/080101.asp.

Lydon, Tom. *ETF Trends*. www.etftrends.com.

Mueller, Jim. *Growth vs. Value: Real Distinction or Not?* The Motley Fool, 2006. www.fool.com/investing/small-cap/2006/04/06/growth-vs-value-real-distinction-or-not.aspx?terms=growth+vs.+value&vstest=search_042607_linkdefault.

Securities and Exchange Commission. *Microcap Stock: A Guide for Investors*. www.sec.gov/investor/pubs/microcapstock.htm.

Whistler, Mark. *Determining What Market Cap Suits Your Style*. Investopedia. www.investopedia.com/articles/mutualfund/06/mfmarketcaps.asp.

Wilcox, Cort. *Growth vs. Value: What's the Difference?* CDAPress.com, 2007. www.postfallspress.com/articles/2007/07/08/business/bus03.txt.

Chapter 4

Citi. *Citi Depositary Receipt Services*. http://wwss.citissb.com/adr/www/index.htm.

Dawson, Chester. "Emerging Markets: Beyond the Big Four." *BusinessWeek*, 2006. www.businessweek.com/magazine/content/05_52/b3965450.htm.

ETF Trends. *What Constitutes an Emerging Market?* www.etftrends.com/emerging_markets/index.html.

ING. *Investing Globally—A World of Opportunity*. www.ingfunds.com.

Kamlet, Art, and George Regnery. *Stocks—American Depositary Receipts ADRs*. The Investment FAQ. http://invest-faq.com/articles/stock-adrs.html.

Larson, Paul. *What Every Would-Be Investor Should Know about China*. Morningstar, 2007. http://news.morningstar.com/forbidden/smartarticleslogin2.html?vurl=http%3a%2f%2fnews.morningstar.com%2farticlenet%2farticle.aspx%3fid%3d195899&referid=A1598.

Maiello, Michael, and Megan Johnson. *2006 Mutual Fund Survey*. Forbes.com. www.forbes.com/free_forbes/2006/0918/142_2.html.

Morningstar. *International Investing Center*. www.morningstar.com/centers/global.html?t1=1184862607&t1=1184944068.

People's Daily Online. *Beijing's Goal: 18 Million People by 2020*. http://english.peopledaily.com.cn/200411/09/eng20041109_163279.html.

Rocco, William Samuel. *Five Steps to Better International Investing*. Morningstar, 2007. http://news.morningstar.com/articlenet/article.aspx?id=189479&_qsbpa=y&globalcsection=moreinfo5&t1=1192555065.

Rosevear, John. *Global Investing Made Simple*. The Motley Fool, 2007. www.fool.com/investing/international/2007/07/19/global-investing-made-simple.aspx.

Skala, Martin. "ETFs: Low-Cost Way to Invest Abroad." *Christian Science Monitor*, 2005. www.csmonitor.com/2005/1006/p16s01-wmgn.html.

Siegel, Aaron. "Investors Think Globally, Invest Locally". *Investment News, 2007*. www.investmentnews.com/apps/pbcs.dll/article?AID=/20070717/REG/70717019/-1/INDaily01.

Van Eck Global. *Market Vectors Russia ETF Handbook*.

Vardy, Nicholas. *Global Investing: Easy As American Pie*. Seeking Alpha, 2007. http://seekingalpha.com/article/25614-global-investing-easy-as-american-pie.

Wikipedia. *Emerging Markets*. http://en.wikipedia.org/wiki/Emerging_markets.

Wikipedia. *The Global Economy*. http://en.wikipedia.org/wiki/the_global_economy.

Xinhua. *Beijing's Population Nears 15 Million*. www.chinadaily.com.cn/english/doc/2005-04/15/content_434469.htm.

Chapter 5

Abnormal Returns. *Cramer on ETF Proliferation*, 2006. www.abnormalreturns.com/2006/07/12/cramer-on-etf-proliferation/.

ChartwellETFAdvisor.com. www.chartwelletfadvisor.com/.

CNNMoney.com. *Top Sector ETFs*. http://money.cnn.com/data/funds/etf/topsectors/.

CNNMoney.com. Various. www.cnnmoney.com.

Culloton, Dan. *Sector ETFs: Use at Your Own Risk*. Morningstar, 2006. http://news.morningstar.com/articlenet/article.aspx?id=166206&_qsbpa=y.

Delfeld, Carl. *Are HealthShares ETFs Too Specialized?* Chartwell Advisor at Seeking Alpha, 2007. http://seekingalpha.com/article/35024-are-healthshares-etfs-too-specialized.

ETFTrends.com. *Healthcare Category*. www.etftrends.com/healthcare/index.html.

Feldman, Jeffery L. *Interactive Q&A: Jeffrey L. Feldman*. 2007. http://seekingalpha.com/article/31559-interactive-q-a-jeffrey-l-feldman-creator-of-healthshares-and-founder-and-chairman-of-xshares-group-llc.

Kathman, David. *Five Tips for Smart Sector Investing*. Morningstar, 2007. http://news.morningstar.com/articlenet/article.aspx?id=185615.

McClatchy, Will. *Specialty Medical ETFs*. ETFZone at Forbes.com, 2007. www.forbes.com/etfs/2007/04/05/xshares-healthshares-medical-pf-etf-in_wm_0404soapbox_inl.html.

Nusbaum, Roger. *Ride the Commodities Bull with ETFs*. TheStreet.com, 2006. www.thestreet.com/etf/etf/10263400.html.

Portfolio Solutions. *The Mutual Fund Follies*. www.portfoliosolutions.com/v2/pdf/Chapter10.pdf.

Richards, Meg. "Sector ETFs Allow Investing in Trends." *Washington Post*, 2005. www.washingtonpost.com/wp-dyn/articles/A20447-2005Apr2.html.

Smart Money. *Are ETFs Right for You?* www.smartmoney.com/etf/education/index.cfm?story=right2004.

Steinhilber, J. D. *ETFs: Broadening or Perverting Index Investing*. Agile Investing, 2007. http://seekingalpha.com/article/27408-etfs-broadening-or-perverting-index-investing.

Taulli, Tom. *Playing Commodities with ETFs*. The Motley Fool, 2005. www.fool.com/news/mft/2005/mft05042908.htm.

Van Schyndel, Zoe. *The ABCs of Currency ETFs*. The Motley Fool, 2006. www.fool.com/investing/etf/2006/08/15/the-abcs-of-currency-etfs.aspx.

Chapter 6

Hamilton, Adam. *Gold ETF Impact*. ZEAL Speculation and Investment, 2006. www.zealllc.com/2006/gldetf.htm.

Investopedia. *Definition of Commodity*. www.investopedia.com/terms/c/commodity.asp.

Lydon, Tom. *New Commodities ETF—Investing in Futures*. ETF Trends, 2006. www.etftrends.com/2006/02/new_commodities.html.

Morris, Sonya. *Avoid These ETFs*. Morningstar, 2006, http://advisor.morningstar.com/articles/doc.asp?docId=12417.

National Mining Association. *Investing in Gold: Introduction and General Overview of Markets*. www.nma.org/statistics/gold/gold_investing.asp.

Oxford Futures. *A Brief History of Commodities*. www.oxfordfutures.com/futures-education/futures-fundamentals/brief-history.htm.

RB Trading. www.rb-trading.com/.

Schoen, John W. *Should I Invest in Commodities?* MSNBC. www.msnbc.msn.com/id/15768192/.

Schwartz, Nelson D. *Why Gas Prices Dropped*. CNNMoney.com, 2006. http://money.cnn.com/magazines/fortune/fortune_archive/2006/10/30/8391681/index.htm.

Seeking Alpha, *Commodity ETFs and ETNs*. 2007. http://seekingalpha.com/article/30369-commodity-etfs-and-etns.

Waldock, Lind. *History of Commodities Exchanges*. www.lind-waldock.com/edu/com/com_history.shtml.

Wikipedia. *Commodity Markets*. http://en.wikipedia.org/wiki/
Commodity_markets.

The returns on inflation, stocks, and bonds are from *Stocks, Bonds,
Bills, and Inflation: The 2007 Yearbook Classic Edition* (Ibbotson
Associates, Morningstar, 2007). This is an indispensable volume on
market history going back to 1926.

The performance data on gold comes from the Bloomberg
professional service.

Chapter 7

Carrel, Lawrence. *More Currency ETFs to Debut*. SmartMoney,
2006. www.smartmoney.com/etffocus/index.cfm?story=20060621.

Experiments in Finance. *Diversifying into Real Estate through REIT
ETFs*. 2006. www.experiglot.com/2006/10/26/diversifying-into-real-
estate-through-reit-etfs.

Federal Reserve Bank of Chicago. *Strong Dollar, Weak Dollar*.
www.chicagofed.org/consumer_information/strong_dollar_
weak_dollar.cfm.

Lydon, Tom. *Currency ETFs as an Asset Class*. ETF Trends, 2006.
www.etftrends.com/2006/09/currency_etfs_a.html.

Pasternak, Carla. *Why Are Income ETFs Taking Off?* Street
Authority, 2004. www.streetauthority.com/cmnts/cp/2004/04-05.asp.

Russell, Michael. *How Are Currency Values Determined?* EZine
Articles. http://ezinearticles.com/?How-are-Currency-Values-
Determined?&id=467643.

Wikipedia. *Currency*. http://en.wikipedia.org/wiki/Currency.

Wood, Carol A. *Real Estate Plays, Hassle-Free. BusinessWeek*, 2005. www.businessweek.com/investor/content/jul2005/pi20050721_3055_pi051.htm.

The inspiration for the supermodel story was "Bündchen Proves Buffett-Savvy Paring Currency Risk," by Adriana Brasileiro (Bloomberg News, November 12, 2007). The piece was picked up all over the world and highlighted the dollar's woes.

Chapter 8

Braun, Martin Z. *Barclays Debuts State-Specific Exchange Traded Funds*. Bloomberg Press, 2007. www.bloomberg.com/apps/news?pid=20601015&sid=a84uqZiGB2Oc&refer=munibonds.

Dow Jones Indexes. *Corporate Bond Index*. www.djindexes.com/mdsidx/?event=showCorpBond.

Investopedia. *Bond ETFs: A Viable Alternative*. 2005. www.investopedia.com/articles/bonds/05/011105.asp.

Investopedia. *Junk Bonds: Everything You Need to Know*. www.investopedia.com/articles/02/052202.asp.

Jackson, David. *Are Bond ETFs a Good Deal?* Seeking Alpha, 2005. http://seekingalpha.com/article/655-are-bond-etfs-a-good-deal.

Krantz, Matt. *Now Is a Good Time to Buy Bonds, but Make Sure You Understand Them*. USA Today, 2006. www.usatoday.com/money/perfi/columnist/krantz/2006-06-06-bonds_x.htm.

MSN Money. *State Street Launches First International Treasury Bond ETF*. 2007. http://news.moneycentral.msn.com/provider/providerarticle.aspx?feed=BW&date=20071005&id=7587309.

Radical Guides. *The Radical Guide to Bonds*. www.radicalguides.com/2005/06/the_radical_gui_1.html.

Van Schyndel, Zoe. *Fixed-Income Fever*. The Motley Fool, 2007. www.fool.com/investing/etf/2007/04/04/fixed-income-fever.aspx.

Chapter 9

Appleby, Denise. *ETFs for Your 401(k)*. Investopedia, 2007. www.forbes.com/personalfinance/retirementcollege/2007/07/25/etfs-401k-iras-pf-education-in_da_0725investopedia_inl.html.

Bell, Heather. *XShares Launches First Lifecycle ETFs*. IndexUniverse, 2007. www.indexuniverse.com/index.php?option=com_content&view=article&id=3172&Itemid=29.

Carrel, Lawrence. *ETF-Only 401k Plans*. Smart Money, 2006. www.smartmoney.com/etffocus/index.cfm?story=20060531.

Consumer Reports. *Investing: A Bargain Alternative to Mutuals*. 2007. www.consumerreports.org/cro/money/personal-investing/exchangetraded-funds-9-07/overview/0709_investing_ov_1.htm?resultPageIndex=1&resultIndex=1&searchTerm=etfs.

Culloton, Dan. *A Surprise Entry in the Race for Actively Managed ETFs*. Morningstar, 2007. http://news.morningstar.com/articlenet/article.aspx?id=193350&_QSBPA=Y&etfsection=Comm4&t1=1187276492.

ETF Trends. *Actively Managed Category*. www.etftrends.com/actively_managed_/index.html.

ETF Trends. *Retirement Category*. www.etftrends.com/retirement/index.html.

Fund Spy. *The Best ETFs for Your IRA*. MSN Money, 2006. http://moneycentral.msn.com/content/invest/mstar/P147804.asp.

Ghosh, Palash R. "ETFs' Goal: 401(k) Plans." *BusinessWeek*, 2005. www.businessweek.com/investor/content/may2005/pi20050519_2637_pi024.htm.

Hansard, Sara. *401(k)s Not Enough for Young Workers*. 2007. www.investmentnews.com/apps/pbcs.dll/article?AID=/20071211/REG/71211006 (based on a GAO report found at http://edlabor.house.gov/publications/401k-GAO-Report-Low-Savings.pdf).Investorwords. *Definition of Collective Trust*. www.investorwords.com/5462/collective_trust.html.

Lancellotta, Amy B. R. *Actively Managed Exchange Traded Funds*. Investment Company Institute, 2002. www.ici.org/statements/cmltr/02_sec_etfs_com.html#TopOfPage.

Reeves, Scott. "ETFs for Retirement." *Forbes*, 2005. www.forbes.com/retirement/2005/06/22/etf-retirement-investing-cx_sr_0622etf.html.

Scherzer, Lisa. *An Evolution in ETFs*. SmartMoney, 2006. www.smartmoney.com/theproshop/index.cfm?Story=20060216.

Spence, John. *New ETFs Target Retirement Market*. MarketWatch, 2007. www.marketwatch.com/news/story/story.aspx?guid=%7B529D466D-F123-483A-B943-C0EECE97A966%7D&siteid=rss.

Stein, Ben. *Anticipating All the Retirement Variables*. Yahoo! Finance, 2007. http://finance.yahoo.com/expert/article/yourlife/43552.

TDAX Funds. *TDAX Funds FAQ*. www.tdaxshares.com/content/view/39/116/#faq6.

TDAX Funds. *TDAX Independence 2040 Overview*. www.
tdaxshares.com/component/option,com_xshares/Itemid,175/
task,viewetf/etfid,16/.

Tiburon Strategic Advisors. *Tiburon Conference PowerPoint Presentation on Retirement*.

Wherry, Rob. "Are Actively Managed ETFs Worth the Wait?" *SmartMoney*, 2007. www.smartmoney.com/fundinsight/index.cfm? story=20070719&src=fb&nav=RSS20.

Yahoo! Finance. *Vanguard Renews Cost Competition in ETF Market with Introduction of Europe Pacific ETF*. Vanguard Press Release, 2007.

Chapter 10

American Stock Exchange. *FAQ*. www.amex.com/?href=/etf/ FAQ/et_etffaq.htm.

Business Wire. *ProShares ETFs Pass $7 Billion in Assets*. 2007. www.businesswire.com/portal/site/google/index.jsp?ndmViewId= news_view&newsId=20070809005029&newsLang=en.

Caplinger, Dan. *The Long and Short of Playing Both Sides*. The Motley Fool, 2007. www.fool.com/investing/mutual-funds/2007/01/ 11/the-long-and-short-of-playing-both-sides.aspx.

Investopedia. *Margin Trading: What Is Buying on Margin?* www.investopedia.com/university/margin/margin1.asp.

McCall, Matthew. *Hedge Against Corrections with Short ETFs*. Investopedia, 2007. http://research.investopedia.com/news/IA/2007/ Hedge_Against_Corrections_With_Short_ETFs.aspx.

Morris, Sonya. *Avoid These ETFs*. Morningstar, 2006. http://news.morningstar.com/articlenet/article.aspx?id=174240&_qsbpa=y.

Wikipedia. *Short Finance*. http://en.wikipedia.org/wiki/Short_selling.

Chapter 11

Fierce Finance. *The Future of ETFs*. 2007. www.fiercefinance.com/story/the-future-of-etfs/2007-04-10.

Investopedia. *Exchange Traded Notes—An Alternative to ETFs*. 2006. www.investopedia.com/articles/06/ETNvsETF.asp.

Lydon, Tom. *The Past and Future of ETFs*. ETF Trends, 2007. www.etftrends.com/2007/08/as-etfs-prolife.html.

Nusbaum, Roger. *The Future of ETFs*. Random Roger, 2005. http://seekingalpha.com/article/628-the-future-of-etfs.

Spence, John. *Barclays' Currency ETNs Dealt a Blow on Taxes*. MarketWatch, 2007. www.marketwatch.com/news/story/story.aspx?guid=%7B1C874197%2D7CAA%2D463B%2DA700%2DA3B15DD1263F%7D&siteid=rss.

Spence, John. *ETNs Face Taxing Times: Lineup of ETF-Like Products Grows, but Tax Advantages in Question*. MarketWatch, 2007. www.marketwatch.com/news/story/tax-advantages-etn-investments-question/story.aspx?guid=%7BB54182F3-3946-4CC0-A7A5-73DAE68D45CB%7D.

Spence, John. *Trouble in ETF Paradise?* MarketWatch, 2007. www.marketwatch.com/news/story/buyer-beware-etf-strategies-become/story.aspx?guid=%7B5C10BD7B%2D4E22%2D4C1F%2D873A%2D680811FF2298%7D.

Wiandt, Jim. *Heavy-Hitting ETFs Could Be the Industry's Ticket*. IndexUniverse, 2005. www.marketwatch.com/News/Story/Story.aspx?
guid=%7BB1D7B090%2D2E02%2D49C8%2DB2DF%2D6C8D5F
7982C2%7D&dist=rss&siteid=mktw.

For the latest on new ETFs, see www.efttrends.com. The ETF of
ETFs product was featured in a November 17, 2007, Wall Street
Journal piece, "Coming Soon: ETFs within ETFs," by Ian Salisbury.

Chapter 12

The Big Picture, *100 Year Dow Jones Industrials Chart*. 2005. http://
bigpicture.typepad.com/comments/2005/12/100_year_bull_b.html.

Bloch, Brian. *Market Timing Fails as a Money Maker*. Investopedia,
2007. www.investopedia.com/articles/trading/07/market_timing.asp.

BusinessWeek. "ETF Strategies for Long-Term Investors." 2004.
http://72.14.253.104/search?q=cache:ONtbGluoG7IJ:www.business
week.com/adsections/2004/pdf/0445_etf.pdf+etf+strategies&hl=en&
ct=clnk&cd=6&gl=us&client=firefox-a.

Charles Schwab. *Schwab's Approach to Asset Allocation*.
www.schwab.com/public/schwab/home/account_types/college_
custodial/529/schwab_asset_allocation.html.

Early, James. *The Pitfalls of ETFs*. The Motley Fool, www.fool.com/
etf/etf04.htm.

InvestorGuide. *Sector ETF Rotation Strategies*. www.investorguide.
com/igu-article-984-etfs-sector-etf-rotation-strategies.html.

Kennon, Joshua. *Asset Allocation*. About.com. http://beginnersinvest.
about.com/od/assetallocation1/a/aa102404.htm.

Learn Money. *A Slightly Different Picture on Wall Street*. 2005. www.learnmoney.co.uk/newsletter/may-2005-2.html.

Legg Mason. *Trend Following*. 2004. http://72.14.253.104/search?q= cache:Z13_C-8eI6UJ:www.trendfollowing.com/legg-mason.pdf+ investing+%22trend+following%22&hl=en&ct=clnk&cd=3&gl= us&client=firefox-a.

Lydon, Tom. *Screening the ETF World*. ETF Trends, 2007. www.etftrends.com/2007/05/how_we_invest_i.html.

MarketScreen. *Moving Averages*. www.marketscreen.com/help/ atoz/default.asp?Num=67.

Masonson, Leslie N. *All About Market Timing*. (New York: McGraw-Hill, 2004).

McWhinney, Jim. *Active vs. Passive Investing in ETFs*. Investopedia, 2006. www.investopedia.com/articles/mutualfund/05/ activepassive.asp.

McWhinney, Jim. *How to Use ETFs in Your Portfolio*. Investopedia, 2005. www.investopedia.com/articles/mutualfund/05/etfstrategy.asp.

The Motley Fool. *ETFs: A 60-Second Guide*. www.fool.com/etf/ etf.htm?source=InvAg.

Rydex Investments. *Dow Jones Historical Trends*. www.portstrat. com/psi_intranet/401(k)_Sidebar/Dow%20Jones%20Historical% 20Chart.%202007.pdf.

Securities and Exchange Commission. *Beginners' Guide to Asset Allocation, Diversification, and Rebalancing*. www.sec.gov/investor/ pubs/assetallocation.htm.

SmartMoney. *No Margin for Error*. www.smartmoney.com/ university/Investing101/stocks/index.cfm?story=20000517.

Street Authority. *Buy and Hold*. www.streetauthority.com/terms/b/
buy-and-hold.asp.

Trade Station. *Risks of Active Trading*. www.tradestation.com/
disclaimers/risks.htm.

Updegrave, Walter. *ETFs: Five Smart Strategies*. CNNMoney.com,
2006. http://money.cnn.com/magazines/moneymag/moneymag_
archive/2006/05/01/8375746/index.htm.

Wachovia Bank, *Risk Calculator—What's Your Sleep Factor?*
www.wachovia.com/personal/calc/women_sleep.

For a classic view on investing, we relied upon Burton Malkiel's
A Random Walk Down Wall Street (W.W. Norton, 2003), which has
been continuously in print since 1973.

Resources

Books

Appel, Marvin. *Investing with Exchange Traded Funds Made Easy: Higher Returns with Lower Costs—Do-It-Yourself Strategies Without Paying Fund Managers*. FT Press, 2007. This primer focuses on technical ways to buy ETFs.

Bernstein, William. *The Four Pillars of Investing: Lessons for Building a Winning Portfolio*. McGraw-Hill, 2002. A classic on building a sensible portfolio.

Bogle, John C. *The Little Book of Common Sense Investing: The Only Way to Guarantee Your Fair Share of Stock Market Returns*. Wiley, 2007. This condensed version of the wisdom of John Bogle is a little gem.

Culloton, Dan, (Introduction) Morningstar Inc. *Morningstar ETFs 150*. Morningstar/Wiley, 2007. Featuring a brief introduction, the book features top ETF funds with the patented Morningstar screens.

Hebner, Mark. *Index Funds: The 12-Step Program for Active Investors*. IFA Publishing, 2007. More than you'd ever want to know about indexing with portfolios dominated by the IFA group.

Lofton, Todd. *Getting Started in Exchange Traded Funds*. Wiley, 2007. A reasonably accessible primer on the subject.

Richards, Archie M., Jr. *Understanding Exchange Traded Funds.*
McGraw-Hill, 2007. A useful resource in exploring the subject.

Services

Bloomberg Professional Service. Geared toward active market pros,
this single platform tracks all listed and future ETFs through its
EXTF function, among thousands of other functions.

Websites

www.efttrends.com. The quintessential resource and blog on ETFs.

www.eftzone.com. ETF articles, commentary, and fund listings from
a number of sources.

www.indexinvestor.com. A good source on indexing with sample
portfolios.

www.indexuniverse.com. News and features on ETFs with a good
column by Jim Wiandt.

www.ici.org. The Investment Company Institute is the trade association for mutual funds but has some information on ETFs.

www.seekingalpha.com. Although not entirely focused on ETFs, this
is a good resource on indexing.

http://finance.yahoo.com/etf. Yahoo! Finance's ETF Center. A sub-
section of the web portal that features news and research on ETFs.

List of ETFs as of November 27, 2007

Name	Ticker	Morningstar Category	Total Assets $MM
Adelante Shares RE Classic ETF	ACK	Specialty-Real Estate	2
Adelante Shares RE Composite ETF	ACB	Specialty-Real Estate	4
Adelante Shares RE Growth ETF	AGV	Specialty-Real Estate	2
Adelante Shares RE Kings ETF	AKB	Specialty-Real Estate	4
Adelante Shares RE Shelter ETF	AQS	Specialty-Real Estate	2
Adelante Shares RE Value ETF	AVU	Specialty-Real Estate	2
Adelante Shares RE Yield Plus ETF	ATY	Specialty-Real Estate	2
Ameristock/Ryan 1 Year Treasury ETF	GKA	Short Government	3
Ameristock/Ryan 10 Year Treasury ETF	GKD	Long Government	3
Ameristock/Ryan 2 Year Treasury ETF	GKB	Short Government	3
Ameristock/Ryan 20 Year Treasury ETF	GKE	Long Government	3
Ameristock/Ryan 5 Year Treasury ETF	GKC	Intermediate Government	3
B2B Internet HOLDRs	BHH	Specialty-Technology	3
Biotech HOLDRs	BBH	Specialty-Health	815
BLDRS Asia 50 ADR Index	ADRA	Diversified Pacific/Asia	123
BLDRS Developed Markets 100 ADR Index	ADRD	Foreign Large Blend	183
BLDRS Emerging Markets 50 ADR Index	ADRE	Diversified Emerging Mkts	911
BLDRS Europe 100 ADR Index	ADRU	Europe Stock	50
Broadband HOLDRs	BDH	Specialty-Technology	63
Claymore S&P Global Water	CGW	Specialty-Natural Res	363
Claymore/BBD High Income	LVL	Large Blend	4
Claymore/BNY BRIC	EEB	Diversified Emerging Mkts	1,052
Claymore/Clear Global Exchanges, Brokers	EXB	Specialty-Financial	54
Claymore/Clear Global Timber Index	CUT	Specialty-Natural Res	19
Claymore/Clear Spin-Off	CSD	Mid-Cap Blend	35

Name	Ticker	Morningstar Category	Total Assets $MM
Claymore/Great Companies Large-Cap Gr	XGC	Large Growth	5
Claymore/Morningstar Info Super Sector	MZN	Large Blend	4
Claymore/Morningstar Mfg Super Sector	MZG	Large Blend	4
Claymore/Morningstar Svc Super Sector	MZO	Large Blend	4
Claymore/Ocean Tomo Growth	OTR	Large Growth	3
Claymore/Ocean Tomo Patent	OTP	Large Blend	11
Claymore/Robb Report Global Luxury	ROB	World Stock	10
Claymore/Robeco Developed Intl Equity	EEN	Foreign Large Blend	5
Claymore/Sabrient Defender	DEF	Large Blend	27
Claymore/Sabrient Insider	NFO	Mid-Cap Blend	28
Claymore/Sabrient Stealth	STH	Small Blend	13
Claymore/SWM Canadian Energy Income	ENY	Specialty-Natural Res	31
Claymore/Zacks Country Rotation	CRO	Foreign Large Blend	5
Claymore/Zacks Dividend Rotation	IRO	Large Blend	3
Claymore/Zacks International Yield Hog	HGI	Foreign Large Blend	9
Claymore/Zacks Mid-Cap Core	CZA	Mid-Cap Blend	5
Claymore/Zacks Sector Rotation	XRO	Large Blend	116
Claymore/Zacks Yield Hog	CVY	Large Blend	62
Consumer Discretionary SPDR	XLY	Large Blend	711
Consumer Staples Select Sector SPDR	XLP	Large Blend	2,186
CurrencyShares Australian Dollar Trust	FXA	World Bond	234
CurrencyShares British Pound Sterling Tr	FXB	World Bond	120
CurrencyShares Canadian Dollar Trust	FXC	World Bond	208
CurrencyShares Euro Trust	FXE	World Bond	981
CurrencyShares Japanese Yen Trust	FXY	World Bond	988
CurrencyShares Mexican Peso Trust	FXM	World Bond	18
CurrencyShares Swedish Krona Trust	FXS	World Bond	54
CurrencyShares Swiss Franc Trust	FXF	World Bond	225
DIAMONDS Trust, Series 1	DIA	Large Value	8,574

Name	Ticker	Morningstar Category	Total Assets $MM
DJ Euro STOXX 50 ETF	FEZ	Europe Stock	531
DJ STOXX 50 ETF	FEU	Europe Stock	161
DJ Wilshire REIT ETF	RWR	Specialty-Real Estate	1,236
ELEMENTS DJ High Yield Select 10 ETN	DOD	Large Value	7
ELEMENTS Morningstar Wide Moat Focus ETN	WMW	Large Blend	5
ELEMENTS Rogers Intl Commodity Agric ETN	RJA	Specialty-Natural Res	61
ELEMENTS Rogers Intl Commodity Enrgy ETN	RJN	Specialty-Natural Res	6
ELEMENTS Rogers Intl Commodity ETN	RJI	Specialty-Natural Res	35
ELEMENTS Rogers Intl Commodity Metal ETN	RJZ	Specialty-Natural Res	5
ELEMENTS SPECTRUM Lg Cap U.S. Sector ETN	EEH	Large Blend	11
Energy Select Sector SPDR	XLE	Specialty-Natural Res	6,996
Europe 2001 HOLDRs	EKH	Europe Stock	25
Fidelity Nasdaq Composite Index Tracking	ONEQ	Large Growth	114
Financial Select Sector SPDR	XLF	Specialty-Financial	5,052
First Trust AMEX Biotechnology Index	FBT	Specialty-Health	73
First Trust Consumer Disc AlphaDEX	FXD	Mid-Cap Growth	2
First Trust Consumer Staples AlphaDEX	FXG	Mid-Cap Value	3
First Trust DB Strategic Value Index	FDV	Large Value	62
First Trust DJ Global Select Dividend	FGD	World Stock	3
First Trust DJ STOXX Select Dividend 30	FDD	Europe Stock	15
First Trust Dow Jones Internet Index	FDN	Specialty-Technology	36
First Trust Dow Jones Select MicroCap	FDM	Small Blend	18

Name	Ticker	Morningstar Category	Total Assets $MM
First Trust Energy AlphaDEX	FXN	Specialty-Natural Res	6
First Trust Financials AlphaDEX	FXO	Specialty-Financial	2
First Trust FTSE EPRA/NAREIT Glb Real Es	FFR	Specialty-Real Estate	5
First Trust Health Care AlphaDEX	FXH	Specialty-Health	2
First Trust Indust/Producer Dur AlphaDEX	FXR	Mid-Cap Blend	5
First Trust IPOX-100 Index	FPX	Large Growth	27
First Trust ISE Chindia	FNI	Pacific/Asia ex-Japan Stk	104
First Trust ISE Water	FIW	Specialty-Natural Res	12
First Trust ISE-Revere Natural Gas	FCG	Specialty-Natural Res	11
First Trust Large Cap Core AlphaDEX	FEX	Large Blend	13
First Trust Large Cap Gr Opp AlphaDEX	FTC	Large Growth	9
First Trust Large Cap Value Opp AlphaDEX	FTA	Large Value	5
First Trust Materials AlphaDEX	FXZ	Specialty-Natural Res	3
First Trust Mid Cap Core AlphaDEX	FNX	Mid-Cap Blend	6
First Trust Morningstar Div Leaders Idx	FDL	Large Value	65
First Trust Multi Cap Growth AlphaDEX	FAD	Mid-Cap Growth	6
First Trust Multi Cap Value AlphaDEX	FAB	Mid-Cap Value	8
First Trust NASDAQ Clean Edge US Liquid	QCLN	Specialty-Natural Res	51
First Trust NASDAQ-100 Equal Weight Idx	QQEW	Large Blend	31
First Trust NASDAQ-100 Ex-Tech Sector	QQXT	Large Blend	2
First Trust NASDAQ-100-Tech Index	QTEC	Specialty-Technology	24
First Trust S&P REIT	FRI	Specialty-Real Estate	2
First Trust Small Cap Core AlphaDEX	FYX	Small Blend	5
First Trust Technology AlphaDEX	FXL	Specialty-Technology	4
First Trust Utilities AlphaDEX	FXU	Specialty-Utilities	1
First Trust Value Line 100 ETF	FVL	Mid-Cap Growth	2
First Trust Value Line Dividend Index	FVD	Large Value	180

Name	Ticker	Morningstar Category	Total Assets $MM
First Trust Value Line Equity Allc Index	FVI	Mid-Cap Blend	13
FocusShares ISE Homebuilders Index	SAW	Large Blend	10
FocusShares ISE SINdex	PUF	Large Blend	4
FocusShares ISE-CCM Homeland Security	MYP	Large Blend	4
FocusShares ISE-Revere Wal-Mart Supplier	WSI	Large Blend	5
Health Care Select Sector SPDR	XLV	Specialty-Health	2,446
HealthShares Autoimmune-Inflammation	HHA	Specialty-Health	2
HealthShares Cancer	HHK	Specialty-Health	10
HealthShares Cardio Devices	HHE	Specialty-Health	5
HealthShares Cardiology	HRD	Specialty-Health	2
HealthShares Composite	HHQ	Specialty-Health	5
HealthShares Dermatology & Wound Care	HRW	Specialty-Health	2
HealthShares Diagnostics	HHD	Specialty-Health	53
HealthShares Emerging Cancer	HHJ	Specialty-Health	5
HealthShares Enabling Technologies	HHV	Specialty-Health	10
HealthShares Euro Medical Prod & Devices	HHT	Specialty-Health	2
HealthShares European Drugs	HRJ	Specialty-Health	2
HealthShares GI/Gender Health	HHU	Specialty-Health	2
HealthShares Infectious Disease	HHG	Specialty-Health	2
HealthShares Metabolic-Endocrine	HHM	Specialty-Health	2
HealthShares Neuroscience	HHN	Specialty-Health	2
HealthShares Ophthalmology	HHZ	Specialty-Health	2
HealthShares Orthopedic Repair	HHP	Specialty-Health	3
HealthShares Patient Care Services	HHB	Specialty-Health	5
HealthShares Respiratory Pulmonary	HHR	Specialty-Health	2
Industrial Select Sector SPDR	XLI	Large Blend	1,663
Internet Architecture HOLDRs	IAH	Specialty-Technology	96
Internet HOLDRs	HHH	Large Growth	393

Name	Ticker	Morningstar Category	Total Assets $MM
Internet Infrastructure HOLDRs	IIH	Specialty-Technology	50
iPath CBOE S&P 500 BuyWrite Index ETN	BWV	Large Blend	15
iPath DJ AIG Agriculture TR Sub-Idx ETN	JJA	Specialty-Natural Res	68
iPath DJ AIG Copper TR Sub-Idx ETN	JJC	Specialty-Natural Res	9
iPath DJ AIG Energy TR Sub-Idx ETN	JJE	Specialty-Natural Res	13
iPath DJ AIG Grains TR Sub-Idx ETN	JJG	Specialty-Natural Res	40
iPath DJ AIG Ind Metals TR Sub-Idx ETN	JJM	Specialty-Natural Res	31
iPath DJ AIG Livestock TR Sub-Idx ETN	COW	Specialty-Natural Res	12
iPath DJ AIG Natural Gas TR Sub-Idx ETN	GAZ	Specialty-Natural Res	9
iPath DJ AIG Nickel TR Sub-Idx ETN	JJN	Specialty-Natural Res	8
iPath Dow Jones-AIG Commodity Idx TR ETN	DJP	Specialty-Natural Res	2,634
iPath EUR/USD Exchange Rate ETN	ERO	World Bond	93
iPath GBP/USD Exchange Rate ETN	GBB	World Bond	13
iPath JPY/USD Exchange Rate ETN	JYN	World Bond	74
iPath MSCI India Index ETN	INP	Pacific/Asia ex-Japan Stk	1,074
iPath S&P GSCI Crude Oil Tot Ret Idx ETN	OIL	Specialty-Natural Res	72
iPath S&P GSCI Total Return Index ETN	GSP	Specialty-Natural Res	260
iShares Cohen & Steers Realty Majors	ICF	Specialty-Real Estate	2,056
iShares COMEX Gold Trust	IAU	Specialty-Precious Metals	1,481
iShares Dow Jones EPAC Select Dividend	IDV	Foreign Large Blend	44
iShares Dow Jones Select Dividend Index	DVY	Large Value	6,913
iShares Dow Jones Transportation Average	IYT	Mid-Cap Blend	221
iShares Dow Jones U.S. Index	IYY	Large Blend	684

Name	Ticker	Morningstar Category	Total Assets $MM
iShares Dow Jones US Aerospace & Defense	ITA	Mid-Cap Blend	475
iShares Dow Jones US Basic Materials	IYM	Specialty-Natural Res	697
iShares Dow Jones US Broker-Dealers	IAI	Specialty-Financial	166
iShares Dow Jones US Consumer Goods	IYK	Large Blend	380
iShares Dow Jones US Consumer Services	IYC	Large Growth	198
iShares Dow Jones US Energy	IYE	Specialty-Natural Res	1,233
iShares Dow Jones US Financial Sector	IYF	Specialty-Financial	425
iShares Dow Jones US Financial Services	IYG	Specialty-Financial	261
iShares Dow Jones US Healthcare	IYH	Specialty-Health	975
iShares Dow Jones US Healthcare Provider	IHF	Specialty-Health	209
iShares Dow Jones US Home Construction	ITB	Large Blend	215
iShares Dow Jones US Industrial	IYJ	Large Blend	364
iShares Dow Jones US Insurance	IAK	Specialty-Financial	55
iShares Dow Jones US Medical Devices	IHI	Specialty-Health	288
iShares Dow Jones US Oil & Gas Ex Index	IEO	Specialty-Natural Res	190
iShares Dow Jones US Oil Equipment Index	IEZ	Specialty-Natural Res	299
iShares Dow Jones US Pharmaceuticals	IHE	Specialty-Health	89
iShares Dow Jones US Real Estate	IYR	Specialty-Real Estate	1,698
iShares Dow Jones US Regional Banks	IAT	Specialty-Financial	77
iShares Dow Jones US Technology	IYW	Specialty-Technology	1,212
iShares Dow Jones US Telecom	IYZ	Specialty-Communications	856
iShares Dow Jones US Utilities	IDU	Specialty-Utilities	848
iShares FTSE Dvlpd Sm Cap ex-North Amer	IFSM	Foreign Small/Mid Growth	9
iShares FTSE EPRA/NAREIT Asia	IFAS	Specialty-Real Estate	5
iShares FTSE EPRA/NAREIT Europe	IFEU	Specialty-Real Estate	5

Name	Ticker	Morningstar Category	Total Assets $MM
iShares FTSE EPRA/NAREIT Global RE ex-US	IFGL	Specialty-Real Estate	9
iShares FTSE EPRA/NAREIT North America	IFNA	Specialty-Real Estate	5
iShares FTSE NAREIT Industrial/Office	FIO	Specialty-Real Estate	6
iShares FTSE NAREIT Mortgage REITs	REM	Specialty-Real Estate	16
iShares FTSE NAREIT Real Estate 50	FTY	Specialty-Real Estate	18
iShares FTSE NAREIT Residential	REZ	Specialty-Real Estate	4
iShares FTSE NAREIT Retail	RTL	Specialty-Real Estate	6
iShares FTSE/Xinhua China 25 Index	FXI	Pacific/Asia ex-Japan Stk	7,145
iShares iBoxx $ High Yield Corporate Bd	HYG	High Yield Bond	296
iShares iBoxx $ Invest Grade Corp Bond	LQD	Long-Term Bond	3,235
iShares JPMorgan USD Emerg Markets Bond	EMB	Emerging Markets Bond	10
iShares KLD 400 Social Index	DSI	Large Blend	52
iShares KLD Select Social Index	KLD	Large Blend	124
iShares Lehman 1-3 Year Credit Bond	CSJ	Short-Term Bond	211
iShares Lehman 1-3 Year Treasury Bond	SHY	Short Government	9,517
iShares Lehman 10-20 Year Treasury Bond	TLH	Long Government	84
iShares Lehman 20+ Year Treasury Bond	TLT	Long Government	1,487
iShares Lehman 3-7 Year Treasury Bond	IEI	Intermediate Government	221
iShares Lehman 7-10 Year Treasury	IEF	Long Government	2,525
iShares Lehman Aggregate Bond	AGG	Intermediate-Term Bond	7,738
iShares Lehman Credit Bond	CFT	Intermediate-Term Bond	50
iShares Lehman Government/ Credit Bond	GBF	Intermediate-Term Bond	41
iShares Lehman Intermediate Govt/Credit Bond	GVI	Intermediate-Term Bond	133
iShares Lehman Intermediate Credit Bond	CIU	Intermediate-Term Bond	110
iShares Lehman MBS Bond	MBB	Intermediate-Term Bond	183
iShares Lehman Short Treasury Bond	SHV	Short-Term Bond	548

Name	Ticker	Morningstar Category	Total Assets $MM
iShares Lehman TIPS Bond	TIP	Inflation-Protected Bond	5,299
iShares Morningstar Large Core Index	JKD	Large Blend	173
iShares Morningstar Large Growth Index	JKE	Large Growth	543
iShares Morningstar Large Value Index	JKF	Large Value	291
iShares Morningstar Mid Core Index	JKG	Mid-Cap Blend	145
iShares Morningstar Mid Growth Index	JKH	Mid-Cap Growth	471
iShares Morningstar Mid Value Index	JKI	Mid-Cap Value	134
iShares Morningstar Small Core Index	JKJ	Small Blend	113
iShares Morningstar Small Growth Index	JKK	Small Growth	86
iShares Morningstar Small Value Index	JKL	Small Value	96
iShares MSCI Australia Index	EWA	Pacific/Asia ex-Japan Stk	1,893
iShares MSCI Austria Index	EWO	Europe Stock	383
iShares MSCI Belgium Index	EWK	Europe Stock	313
iShares MSCI Brazil Index	EWZ	Latin America Stock	7,580
iShares MSCI BRIC Index	BKF	Diversified Emerging Mkts	30
iShares MSCI Canada Index	EWC	Foreign Large Value	1,898
iShares MSCI Chile Index	ECH	Latin America Stock	24
iShares MSCI EAFE Growth Index	EFG	Foreign Large Growth	1,156
iShares MSCI EAFE Index	EFA	Foreign Large Blend	51,895
iShares MSCI EAFE Small Cap Index	SCZ	Foreign Small/Mid Value	10
iShares MSCI EAFE Value Index	EFV	Foreign Large Value	1,188
iShares MSCI Emerging Markets Index	EEM	Diversified Emerging Mkts	28,854
iShares MSCI EMU Index	EZU	Europe Stock	2,904
iShares MSCI France Index	EWQ	Europe Stock	613
iShares MSCI Germany Index	EWG	Europe Stock	1,973
iShares MSCI Hong Kong Index	EWH	Pacific/Asia ex-Japan Stk	2,590
iShares MSCI Italy Index	EWI	Europe Stock	186
iShares MSCI Japan Index	EWJ	Japan Stock	10,313
iShares MSCI Japan Small Cap Index	SCJ	Japan Stock	5
iShares MSCI Kokusai Index	TOK	Foreign Large Blend	10
iShares MSCI Malaysia Index	EWM	Pacific/Asia ex-Japan Stk	1,111

Name	Ticker	Morningstar Category	Total Assets $MM
iShares MSCI Mexico Index	EWW	Latin America Stock	1,209
iShares MSCI Netherlands Index	EWN	Europe Stock	259
iShares MSCI Pacific ex-Japan	EPP	Pacific/Asia ex-Japan Stk	4,105
iShares MSCI Singapore Index	EWS	Pacific/Asia ex-Japan Stk	2,124
iShares MSCI South Africa Index	EZA	Diversified Emerging Mkts	678
iShares MSCI South Korea Index	EWY	Pacific/Asia ex-Japan Stk	3,668
iShares MSCI Spain Index	EWP	Europe Stock	775
iShares MSCI Sweden Index	EWD	Europe Stock	387
iShares MSCI Switzerland Index	EWL	Europe Stock	376
iShares MSCI Taiwan Index	EWT	Pacific/Asia ex-Japan Stk	2,657
iShares MSCI United Kingdom Index	EWU	Europe Stock	1,171
iShares Nasdaq Biotechnology	IBB	Specialty-Health	1,539
iShares NYSE 100 Index	NY	Large Value	106
iShares NYSE Composite Index	NYC	Large Blend	134
iShares Russell 1000 Growth Index	IWF	Large Growth	15,553
iShares Russell 1000 Index	IWB	Large Blend	3,762
iShares Russell 1000 Value Index	IWD	Large Value	10,489
iShares Russell 2000 Growth Index	IWO	Small Growth	3,500
iShares Russell 2000 Index	IWM	Small Blend	11,222
iShares Russell 2000 Value Index	IWN	Small Value	3,982
iShares Russell 3000 Growth Index	IWZ	Large Growth	436
iShares Russell 3000 Index	IWV	Large Blend	2,946
iShares Russell 3000 Value Index	IWW	Large Value	698
iShares Russell Microcap Index	IWC	Small Blend	310
iShares Russell Midcap Growth Index	IWP	Mid-Cap Growth	3,213
iShares Russell Midcap Index	IWR	Mid-Cap Blend	3,934
iShares Russell Midcap Value Index	IWS	Mid-Cap Value	3,050
iShares S&P 100 Index	OEF	Large Blend	4,890
iShares S&P 1500 Index	ISI	Large Blend	228
iShares S&P 500 Growth Index	IVW	Large Growth	6,622
iShares S&P 500 Index	IVV	Large Blend	17,895

Name	Ticker	Morningstar Category	Total Assets $MM
iShares S&P 500 Value Index	IVE	Large Value	4,456
iShares S&P Asia 50 Index	AIA	Diversified Pacific/Asia	14
iShares S&P California Municipal Bond	CMF	Muni California Interm/Sh	42
iShares S&P Europe 350 Index	IEV	Europe Stock	2,891
iShares S&P Global 100 Index	IOO	World Stock	976
iShares S&P Global Cons Discretionary	RXI	World Stock	27
iShares S&P Global Consumer Staples	KXI	World Stock	175
iShares S&P Global Energy	IXC	Specialty-Natural Res	1,057
iShares S&P Global Financials	IXG	Specialty-Financial	243
iShares S&P Global Healthcare	IXJ	Specialty-Health	709
iShares S&P Global Industrials	EXI	World Stock	219
iShares S&P Global Infrastructure Index	IGF	Specialty-Utilities	5
iShares S&P Global Materials	MXI	Specialty-Natural Res	421
iShares S&P Global Technology	IXN	Specialty-Technology	467
iShares S&P Global Telecommunications	IXP	Specialty-Communications	570
iShares S&P Global Utilities	JXI	Specialty-Utilities	180
iShares S&P GSCI Commodity-Indexed Trust	GSG	Specialty-Natural Res	458
iShares S&P GSSI Natural Resources	IGE	Specialty-Natural Res	2,238
iShares S&P GSTI Networking	IGN	Specialty-Technology	167
iShares S&P GSTI Semiconductor	IGW	Specialty-Technology	229
iShares S&P GSTI Software	IGV	Specialty-Technology	418
iShares S&P GSTI Technology	IGM	Specialty-Technology	439
iShares S&P Latin America 40 Index	ILF	Latin America Stock	3,091
iShares S&P MidCap 400 Growth Index	IJK	Mid-Cap Growth	2,314
iShares S&P MidCap 400 Index	IJH	Mid-Cap Blend	4,873
iShares S&P MidCap 400 Value Index	IJJ	Mid-Cap Value	2,394
iShares S&P National Municipal Bond	MUB	Muni National Interm	332
iShares S&P New York Municipal Bond	NYF	Muni New York Interm/Shor	20
iShares S&P SmallCap 600 Growth	IJT	Small Growth	1,489

Name	Ticker	Morningstar Category	Total Assets $MM
iShares S&P SmallCap 600 Index	IJR	Small Blend	4,369
iShares S&P SmallCap 600 Value Index	IJS	Small Value	1,571
iShares S&P U.S. Preferred Stock Index	PFF	Large Blend	68
iShares S&P World ex-US Property Index	WPS	Specialty-Real Estate	59
iShares S&P/TOPIX 150 Index	ITF	Japan Stock	247
iShares Silver Trust	SLV	Specialty-Precious Metals	2,488
KBW Bank ETF	KBE	Specialty-Financial	364
KBW Capital Markets ETF	KCE	Specialty-Financial	158
KBW Insurance ETF	KIE	Specialty-Financial	84
KBW Regional Banking ETF	KRE	Specialty-Financial	57
MACROshares Oil Down Tradeable Shares	DCR	Specialty-Natural Res	12
MACROshares Oil Up Tradeable Shares	UCR	Specialty-Natural Res	48
Market 2000 HOLDRs	MKH	Large Blend	52
Market Vectors Global Agribusiness ETF	MOO	World Stock	706
Market Vectors Global Nuclear Energy ETF	NLR	Specialty-Natural Res	126
Market Vectors Gold Miners ETF	GDX	Specialty-Precious Metals	1,436
Market Vectors Lehman AMT-Free Int Muni	ITM	Muni National Interm	10
Market Vectors Russia ETF	RSX	Diversified Emerging Mkts	800
Market Vectors Steel ETF	SLX	Specialty-Natural Res	251
Materials Select Sector SPDR	XLB	Specialty-Natural Res	1,422
MidCap SPDRs	MDY	Mid-Cap Blend	10,107
Mkt Vectors Environmental Services ETF	EVX	Mid-Cap Blend	36
Mkt Vectors Glb Alternative Energy ETF	GEX	Specialty-Natural Res	238
Morgan Stanley Technology ETF	MTK	Specialty-Technology	266
NYSE Arca Tech 100 ETF	NXT	Specialty-Technology	8
Oil Services HOLDRs	OIH	Specialty-Natural Res	3,626
Pharmaceutical HOLDRs	PPH	Specialty-Health	1,990
PowerShares 1-30 Laddered Treasury	PLW	Long Government	16

Name	Ticker	Morningstar Category	Total Assets $MM
PowerShares Aerospace & Defense	PPA	Large Growth	376
PowerShares Buyback Achievers	PKW	Large Blend	85
PowerShares Cleantech	PZD	Small Growth	114
PowerShares DB Agriculture	DBA	Specialty-Natural Res	1,089
PowerShares DB Base Metals	DBB	Specialty-Natural Res	48
PowerShares DB Commodity Idx Trking Fund	DBC	Specialty-Natural Res	1,535
PowerShares DB Energy	DBE	Specialty-Natural Res	49
PowerShares DB G10 Currency Harvest	DBV	World Bond	515
PowerShares DB Gold	DGL	Specialty-Precious Metals	44
PowerShares DB Oil	DBO	Specialty-Natural Res	35
PowerShares DB Precious Metals	DBP	Specialty-Precious Metals	56
PowerShares DB Silver	DBS	Specialty-Precious Metals	28
PowerShares DB US Dollar Index Bearish	UDN	World Bond	77
PowerShares DB US Dollar Index Bullish	UUP	World Bond	100
PowerShares Dividend Achievers	PFM	Large Value	72
PowerShares DWA Dev Mrkts Technical Ldrs	PIZ	Foreign Large Blend	3
PowerShares DWA Em Mrkts Technical Ldrs	PIE	Foreign Large Blend	5
PowerShares DWA Technical Leaders	PDP	Mid-Cap Blend	317
PowerShares Dynamic Aggressive Growth	PGZ	Mid-Cap Growth	11
PowerShares Dynamic Asia Pacific	PUA	Diversified Pacific/Asia	37
PowerShares Dynamic Banking	PJB	Specialty-Financial	59
PowerShares Dynamic Basic Materials	PYZ	Specialty-Natural Res	38
PowerShares Dynamic Biotech & Genome	PBE	Specialty-Health	243
PowerShares Dynamic Building & Construct	PKB	Large Blend	22
PowerShares Dynamic Consumer Discr	PEZ	Mid-Cap Blend	17

Name	Ticker	Morningstar Category	Total Assets $MM
PowerShares Dynamic Consumer Staples	PSL	Large Blend	16
PowerShares Dynamic Deep Value	PVM	Mid-Cap Value	12
PowerShares Dynamic Developed Intl Opps	PFA	Foreign Large Blend	60
PowerShares Dynamic Energy	PXI	Specialty-Natural Res	36
PowerShares Dynamic Energy Explor & Prod	PXE	Specialty-Natural Res	157
PowerShares Dynamic Europe	PEH	Europe Stock	7
PowerShares Dynamic Financials	PFI	Specialty-Financial	20
PowerShares Dynamic Food & Beverage	PBJ	Large Blend	34
PowerShares Dynamic Hardware & Cons Elec	PHW	Specialty-Technology	16
PowerShares Dynamic Healthcare	PTH	Specialty-Health	102
PowerShares Dynamic Healthcare Services	PTJ	Specialty-Health	56
PowerShares Dynamic Industrials	PRN	Mid-Cap Blend	31
PowerShares Dynamic Insurance	PIC	Specialty-Financial	43
PowerShares Dynamic Large Cap	PJF	Large Blend	22
PowerShares Dynamic Large Cap Growth	PWB	Large Growth	720
PowerShares Dynamic Large Cap Value	PWV	Large Value	269
PowerShares Dynamic Leisure & Entertain	PEJ	Large Blend	19
PowerShares Dynamic MagniQuant	PIQ	Mid-Cap Blend	80
PowerShares Dynamic Market	PWC	Large Blend	771
PowerShares Dynamic Media	PBS	Specialty-Communications	37
PowerShares Dynamic Mid Cap	PJG	Mid-Cap Blend	19
PowerShares Dynamic Mid Cap Growth	PWJ	Mid-Cap Growth	442
PowerShares Dynamic Mid Cap Value	PWP	Mid-Cap Value	98
PowerShares Dynamic Networking	PXQ	Specialty-Technology	20
PowerShares Dynamic Oil & Gas Services	PXJ	Specialty-Natural Res	396
PowerShares Dynamic OTC	PWO	Mid-Cap Growth	127

Name	Ticker	Morningstar Category	Total Assets $MM
PowerShares Dynamic Pharmaceuticals	PJP	Specialty-Health	89
PowerShares Dynamic Retail	PMR	Large Blend	9
PowerShares Dynamic Semiconductors	PSI	Specialty-Technology	90
PowerShares Dynamic Small Cap	PJM	Small Blend	10
PowerShares Dynamic Small Cap Growth	PWT	Small Growth	61
PowerShares Dynamic Small Cap Value	PWY	Small Value	96
PowerShares Dynamic Software	PSJ	Specialty-Technology	56
PowerShares Dynamic Technology	PTF	Specialty-Technology	41
PowerShares Dynamic Telecom & Wireless	PTE	Specialty-Communications	28
PowerShares Dynamic Utilities	PUI	Specialty-Utilities	38
PowerShares Emerging Mkts Sovereign Debt	PCY	Emerging Markets Bond	35
PowerShares Financial Preferred	PGF	Specialty-Financial	128
PowerShares FTSE RAFI Asia Pacific exJpn S/M	PDQ	Pacific/Asia ex-Japan Stk	15
PowerShares FTSE RAFI Asia Pacific ex-Jp	PAF	Pacific/Asia ex-Japan Stk	17
PowerShares FTSE RAFI Basic Materials	PRFM	Specialty-Natural Res	13
PowerShares FTSE RAFI Consumer Goods	PRFG	Large Blend	5
PowerShares FTSE RAFI Consumer Services	PRFS	Large Blend	10
PowerShares FTSE RAFI Developed Mkts ex-US	PXF	Foreign Large Blend	50
PowerShares FTSE RAFI Developed Mkts exUS S/M	PDN	Foreign Small/Mid Growth	10
PowerShares FTSE RAFI Emerging Markets	PXH	Foreign Large Blend	42
PowerShares FTSE RAFI Energy	PRFE	Specialty-Natural Res	23
PowerShares FTSE RAFI Europe	PEF	Europe Stock	10
PowerShares FTSE RAFI Europe Small-Mid	PWD	Europe Stock	7

Name	Ticker	Morningstar Category	Total Assets $MM
PowerShares FTSE RAFI Financials	PRFF	Specialty-Financial	17
PowerShares FTSE RAFI Health Care	PRFH	Specialty-Health	16
PowerShares FTSE RAFI Industrials	PRFN	Large Blend	30
PowerShares FTSE RAFI Intl Real Est ETF	PRY	Specialty-Real Estate	3
PowerShares FTSE RAFI Japan	PJO	Japan Stock	9
PowerShares FTSE RAFI Telecom & Tech	PRFQ	Specialty-Communications	18
PowerShares FTSE RAFI US 1000	PRF	Large Value	981
PowerShares FTSE RAFI US 1500 Small-Mid	PRFZ	Small Blend	123
PowerShares FTSE RAFI Utilities	PRFU	Specialty-Utilities	12
PowerShares Gldn Dragon Halter USX China	PGJ	Pacific/Asia ex-Japan Stk	748
PowerShares Global Clean Energy	PBD	Specialty-Natural Res	141
PowerShares Global Water	PIO	Specialty-Natural Res	263
PowerShares High Growth Rate Div Achiev	PHJ	Large Blend	30
PowerShares High Yield Corporate Bond	PHB	High Yield Bond	5
PowerShares HighYield Dividend Achievers	PEY	Mid-Cap Value	251
PowerShares Insured California Muni Bond	PWZ	Muni California Long	12
PowerShares Insured National Muni Bond	PZA	Muni National Long	15
PowerShares Insured New York Muni Bond	PZT	Muni New York Long	15
PowerShares Intl Dividend Achievers	PID	Foreign Large Value	745
PowerShares Intl Listed Private Equity	PFP	Foreign Large Growth	9
PowerShares Listed Private Equity	PSP	Mid-Cap Blend	124
PowerShares Lux Nanotech	PXN	Specialty-Technology	117
PowerShares QQQ	QQQQ	Large Growth	21,767
PowerShares Value Line Industry Rotation	PYH	Large Blend	42

Name	Ticker	Morningstar Category	Total Assets $MM
PowerShares Value Line Timeliness Select	PIV	Mid-Cap Growth	218
PowerShares VRDO Tax-Free Weekly	PVI	Muni National Short	8
PowerShares Water Resources	PHO	Specialty-Natural Res	2,134
PowerShares WilderHill Clean Energy	PBW	Specialty-Natural Res	1,731
PowerShares WilderHill Prog Energy	PUW	Specialty-Natural Res	57
PowerShares Zacks Micro Cap	PZI	Small Blend	130
PowerShares Zacks Small Cap	PZJ	Small Blend	49
Regional Bank HOLDRs	RKH	Specialty-Financial	553
Retail HOLDRs	RTH	Large Blend	446
Rydex 2x Russell 2000	RRY	Small Blend	10
Rydex 2x S&P 500	RSU	Large Blend	11
Rydex 2x S&P MidCap 400	RMM	Mid-Cap Blend	11
Rydex Inverse 2x Russell 2000	RRZ	Bear Market	12
Rydex Inverse 2x S&P 500	RSW	Bear Market	16
Rydex Inverse 2x S&P MidCap 400	RMS	Bear Market	12
Rydex Russell Top 50	XLG	Large Blend	647
Rydex S&P 500 Pure Growth	RPG	Large Growth	47
Rydex S&P 500 Pure Value	RPV	Large Value	36
Rydex S&P Equal Weight	RSP	Large Blend	1,684
Rydex S&P Equal Weight Consumer Discr	RCD	Large Blend	16
Rydex S&P Equal Weight Consumer Staples	RHS	Large Blend	8
Rydex S&P Equal Weight Energy	RYE	Specialty-Natural Res	17
Rydex S&P Equal Weight Financials	RYF	Specialty-Financial	6
Rydex S&P Equal Weight Health Care	RYH	Specialty-Health	17
Rydex S&P Equal Weight Industrials	RGI	Large Blend	8
Rydex S&P Equal Weight Materials	RTM	Specialty-Natural Res	8
Rydex S&P Equal Weight Technology	RYT	Specialty-Technology	23
Rydex S&P Equal Weight Utilities	RYU	Specialty-Utilities	6
Rydex S&P Midcap 400 Pure Growth	RFG	Mid-Cap Growth	20

Name	Ticker	Morningstar Category	Total Assets $MM
Rydex S&P Midcap 400 Pure Value	RFV	Mid-Cap Value	15
Rydex S&P Smallcap 600 Pure Growth	RZG	Small Growth	6
Rydex S&P Smallcap 600 Pure Value	RZV	Small Value	20
Semiconductor HOLDRs	SMH	Specialty-Technology	1,390
Short Dow30 ProShares	DOG	Bear Market	111
Short MidCap400 ProShares	MYY	Bear Market	45
Short MSCI EAFE ProShares	EFZ	Bear Market	16
Short MSCI Emerging Mrkts ProShares	EUM	Bear Market	16
Short QQQ ProShares	PSQ	Bear Market	68
Short Russell2000 ProShares	RWM	Bear Market	54
Short S&P SmallCap600 ProShares	SBB	Bear Market	11
Short S&P500 ProShares	SH	Bear Market	205
Software HOLDRs	SWH	Specialty-Technology	160
SPA MarketGrader 100	SIH	Large Blend	2
SPA MarketGrader 200	SNB	Large Blend	2
SPA MarketGrader 40	SFV	Large Blend	2
SPA MarketGrader Large Cap 100	SZG	Large Blend	2
SPA MarketGrader Mid Cap 100	SVD	Mid-Cap Blend	2
SPA MarketGrader Small Cap 100	SSK	Small Blend	5
SPDR Barclays Capital TIPS	IPE	Inflation-Protected Bond	30
SPDR DJ Global Titans	DGT	World Stock	189
SPDR DJ Wilshire Intl Real Estate	RWX	Specialty-Real Estate	993
SPDR DJ Wilshire Large Cap	ELR	Large Blend	10
SPDR DJ Wilshire Large Cap Growth	ELG	Large Growth	323
SPDR DJ Wilshire Large Cap Value	ELV	Large Value	120
SPDR DJ Wilshire Mid Cap	EMM	Mid-Cap Blend	22
SPDR DJ Wilshire Mid Cap Growth	EMG	Mid-Cap Growth	46
SPDR DJ Wilshire Mid Cap Value	EMV	Mid-Cap Value	11
SPDR DJ Wilshire Small Cap	DSC	Small Blend	9
SPDR DJ Wilshire Small Cap Growth	DSG	Small Growth	88
SPDR DJ Wilshire Small Cap Value	DSV	Small Value	96

Name	Ticker	Morningstar Category	Total Assets $MM
SPDR DJ Wilshire Total Market	TMW	Large Blend	127
SPDR FTSE/Macquarie Global Infra 100	GII	Specialty-Utilities	73
SPDR Lehman 1-3 Month T-Bill	BIL	Ultrashort Bond	211
SPDR Lehman Aggregate Bond	LAG	Intermediate-Term Bond	64
SPDR Lehman California Municipal Bond	CXA	Muni California Long	13
SPDR Lehman High Yield Bond	JNK	High Yield Bond	9
SPDR Lehman Intermediate Term Treasury	ITE	Intermediate Government	11
SPDR Lehman Intl Treasury Bond ETF	BWX	World Bond	181
SPDR Lehman Long Term Treasury	TLO	Long Government	21
SPDR Lehman Municipal Bond	TFI	Muni National Long	71
SPDR Lehman New York Municipal Bond	INY	Muni New York Long	13
SPDR Lehman Short Term Municipal Bond	SHM	Muni National Short	23
SPDR MSCI ACWI (ex-US)	CWI	Foreign Large Blend	257
SPDR Russell/Nomura PRIME Japan	JPP	Japan Stock	61
SPDR Russell/Nomura Small Cap Japan	JSC	Japan Stock	93
SPDR S&P Biotech	XBI	Specialty-Health	276
SPDR S&P BRIC 40	BIK	Diversified Emerging Mkts	320
SPDR S&P China	GXC	Pacific/Asia ex-Japan Stk	192
SPDR S&P Dividend	SDY	Large Value	234
SPDR S&P Emerging Asia Pacific	GMF	Pacific/Asia ex-Japan Stk	115
SPDR S&P Emerging Europe	GUR	Europe Stock	78
SPDR S&P Emerging Latin America	GML	Latin America Stock	65
SPDR S&P Emerging Markets	GMM	Diversified Emerging Mkts	54
SPDR S&P Emerging Middle East & Africa	GAF	Diversified Emerging Mkts	70
SPDR S&P Homebuilders	XHB	Mid-Cap Value	303
SPDR S&P International Small Cap	GWX	Foreign Small/Mid Growth	258
SPDR S&P Metals & Mining	XME	Specialty-Natural Res	261

Name	Ticker	Morningstar Category	Total Assets $MM
SPDR S&P Oil & Gas Equipment & Services	XES	Specialty-Natural Res	197
SPDR S&P Oil & Gas Exploration & Prod	XOP	Specialty-Natural Res	81
SPDR S&P Pharmaceuticals	XPH	Specialty-Health	8
SPDR S&P Retail	XRT	Mid-Cap Growth	110
SPDR S&P Semiconductor	XSD	Specialty-Technology	163
SPDR S&P World ex-US	GWL	Foreign Large Blend	13
SPDRs	SPY	Large Blend	98,152
streetTRACKS Gold Shares	GLD	Specialty-Precious Metals	16,826
TDAX Independence 2010 ETF	TDD	Target-Date 2000-2014	15
TDAX Independence 2020 ETF	TDH	Target-Date 2015-2029	35
TDAX Independence 2030 ETF	TDN	Target-Date 2030+	25
TDAX Independence 2040 ETF	TDV	Target-Date 2030+	30
TDAX Independence In-Target ETF	TDX	Conservative Allocation	15
Technology Select Sector SPDR	XLK	Specialty-Technology	3,009
Telecom HOLDRs	TTH	Specialty-Communications	187
Ultra Basic Materials ProShares	UYM	Specialty-Natural Res	29
Ultra Consumer Goods ProShares	UGE	Large Blend	6
Ultra Consumer Services ProShares	UCC	Large Blend	4
Ultra Dow30 ProShares	DDM	Large Blend	236
Ultra Financials ProShares	UYG	Specialty-Financial	214
Ultra Health Care ProShares	RXL	Specialty-Health	11
Ultra Industrials ProShares	UXI	Large Blend	12
Ultra MidCap400 ProShares	MVV	Mid-Cap Blend	77
Ultra Oil & Gas ProShares	DIG	Specialty-Natural Res	58
Ultra QQQ ProShares	QLD	Large Blend	892
Ultra Real Estate ProShares	URE	Specialty-Real Estate	16
Ultra Russell MidCap Growth ProShares	UKW	Mid-Cap Growth	20
Ultra Russell MidCap Value Proshares	UVU	Mid-Cap Value	8
Ultra Russell1000 Growth ProShares	UKF	Large Growth	27

Name	Ticker	Morningstar Category	Total Assets $MM
Ultra Russell1000 Value ProShares	UVG	Large Value	9
Ultra Russell2000 Growth ProShares	UKK	Small Growth	10
Ultra Russell2000 ProShares	UWM	Small Blend	77
Ultra Russell2000 Value ProShares	UVT	Small Value	7
Ultra S&P SmallCap600 ProShares	SAA	Small Blend	14
Ultra S&P500 ProShares	SSO	Large Blend	568
Ultra Semiconductor ProShares	USD	Specialty-Technology	32
Ultra Technology ProShares	ROM	Specialty-Technology	61
Ultra Utilities ProShares	UPW	Specialty-Utilities	19
UltraShort Basic Materials ProShares	SMN	Specialty-Natural Res	58
UltraShort Consumer Goods ProShares	SZK	Bear Market	19
UltraShort Consumer Services ProShares	SCC	Bear Market	32
UltraShort Dow30 ProShares	DXD	Bear Market	444
UltraShort Financials ProShares	SKF	Bear Market	967
UltraShort FTSE/Xinhua China 25 Proshare	FXP	Bear Market	374
UltraShort Health Care ProShares	RXD	Bear Market	10
UltraShort Industrials ProShares	SIJ	Bear Market	21
UltraShort MidCap400 ProShares	MZZ	Bear Market	160
Ultrashort MSCI EAFE ProShares	EFU	Bear Market	33
UltraShort MSCI Emerging Mrkts ProShares	EEV	Bear Market	82
UltraShort MSCI Japan ProShares	EWV	Bear Market	11
UltraShort Oil & Gas ProShares	DUG	Bear Market	268
UltraShort QQQ ProShares	QID	Bear Market	1,256
UltraShort Real Estate ProShares	SRS	Bear Market	580
UltraShort Russell MidCap Gr ProShares	SDK	Bear Market	5
UltraShort Russell MidCap Val ProShares	SJL	Bear Market	6
UltraShort Russell1000 Growth ProShares	SFK	Bear Market	19
UltraShort Russell1000 Value ProShares	SJF	Bear Market	6

Name	Ticker	Morningstar Category	Total Assets $MM
UltraShort Russell2000 Growth ProShares	SKK	Bear Market	25
UltraShort Russell2000 ProShares	TWM	Bear Market	604
UltraShort Russell2000 Value ProShares	SJH	Bear Market	33
UltraShort S&P500 ProShares	SDS	Bear Market	1,652
UltraShort Semiconductor ProShares	SSG	Bear Market	9
UltraShort SmallCap600 ProShares	SDD	Bear Market	47
UltraShort Technology ProShares	REW	Bear Market	20
UltraShort Utilities ProShares	SDP	Bear Market	11
United States 12 Month Oil	USL	Specialty-Natural Res	22
United States Natural Gas	UNG	Specialty-Natural Res	3
United States Oil	USO	Specialty-Natural Res	485
Utilities HOLDRs	UTH	Specialty-Utilities	440
Utilities Select Sector SPDR	XLU	Specialty-Utilities	2,504
Vanguard Consumer Discretionary ETF	VCR	Large Growth	133
Vanguard Consumer Staples ETF	VDC	Large Blend	418
Vanguard Dividend Appreciation ETF	VIG	Large Blend	226
Vanguard Emerging Markets Stock ETF	VWO	Diversified Emerging Mkts	5,969
Vanguard Energy ETF	VDE	Specialty-Natural Res	762
Vanguard Europe Pacific ETF	VEA	Foreign Large Blend	653
Vanguard European Stock ETF	VGK	Europe Stock	3,100
Vanguard Extended Dur Tre Idx ETF	EDV	Long Government	15
Vanguard Extended Market Index ETF	VXF	Mid-Cap Blend	559
Vanguard Financials ETF	VFH	Specialty-Financial	406
Vanguard FTSE All-World ex-US ETF	VEU	Foreign Large Blend	1,322
Vanguard Growth ETF	VUG	Large Growth	3,232
Vanguard Health Care ETF	VHT	Specialty-Health	515
Vanguard High Dividend Yield Indx ETF	VYM	Large Value	97
Vanguard Industrials ETF	VIS	Large Blend	242
Vanguard Information Technology ETF	VGT	Specialty-Technology	596
Vanguard Intermediate-Term Bond ETF	BIV	Intermediate-Term Bond	169

Name	Ticker	Morningstar Category	Total Assets $MM
Vanguard Large Cap ETF	VV	Large Blend	1,162
Vanguard Long-Term Bond ETF	BLV	Long-Term Bond	84
Vanguard Materials ETF	VAW	Specialty-Natural Res	344
Vanguard Mega Cap 300 Gr Index ETF	MGK	Large Growth	5
Vanguard Mega Cap 300 Index ETF	MGC	Large Blend	5
Vanguard Mega Cap 300 Value Index ETF	MGV	Large Value	15
Vanguard Mid Cap ETF	VO	Mid-Cap Blend	1,087
Vanguard Mid-Cap Growth ETF	VOT	Mid-Cap Growth	377
Vanguard Mid-Cap Value ETF	VOE	Mid-Cap Value	215
Vanguard Pacific Stock ETF	VPL	Japan Stock	1,414
Vanguard REIT Index ETF	VNQ	Specialty-Real Estate	1,682
Vanguard Short-Term Bond ETF	BSV	Short-Term Bond	407
Vanguard Small Cap ETF	VB	Small Blend	1,121
Vanguard Small Cap Growth ETF	VBK	Small Growth	858
Vanguard Small Cap Value ETF	VBR	Small Value	819
Vanguard Telecom Services ETF	VOX	Specialty-Communications	211
Vanguard Total Bond Market ETF	BND	Intermediate-Term Bond	1,095
Vanguard Total Stock Market ETF	VTI	Large Blend	10,255
Vanguard Utilities ETF	VPU	Specialty-Utilities	335
Vanguard Value ETF	VTV	Large Value	2,215
Wireless HOLDRs	WMH	Specialty-Communications	72
WisdomTree DEFA	DWM	Foreign Large Blend	437
WisdomTree DEFA High-Yielding Equity	DTH	Foreign Large Blend	266
WisdomTree Dividend Top 100	DTN	Large Blend	194
WisdomTree Earnings 500	EPS	Large Blend	56
WisdomTree Earnings Top 100	EEZ	Large Blend	15
WisdomTree Emerging Mkts High-Yielding Eq	DEM	Diversified Emerging Mkts	139
WisdomTree Emerging Mkts Small Cap Div	DGS	Diversified Emerging Mkts	33

Name	Ticker	Morningstar Category	Total Assets $MM
WisdomTree Europe High-Yielding Equity	DEW	Europe Stock	59
WisdomTree Europe SmallCap Dividend	DFE	Europe Stock	67
WisdomTree Europe Total Dividend	DEB	Europe Stock	54
WisdomTree High-Yielding Equity	DHS	Large Blend	144
WisdomTree International Basic Materials	DBN	Specialty-Natural Res	105
WisdomTree International Communications	DGG	Specialty-Communications	43
WisdomTree International Cons Cyclical	DPC	Foreign Large Blend	6
WisdomTree International Cons Non-Cycl	DPN	Foreign Large Blend	30
WisdomTree International Div Top 100	DOO	Foreign Large Blend	487
WisdomTree International Energy	DKA	Specialty-Natural Res	55
WisdomTree International Financial	DRF	Specialty-Financial	21
WisdomTree International Health Care	DBR	Specialty-Health	27
WisdomTree International Industrial	DDI	Foreign Large Blend	46
WisdomTree International LargeCap Div	DOL	Foreign Large Blend	172
WisdomTree International MidCap Dividend	DIM	Foreign Small/Mid Value	236
WisdomTree International Real Estate	DRW	Specialty-Real Estate	106
WisdomTree International SmallCap Div	DLS	Foreign Small/Mid Value	576
WisdomTree International Technology	DBT	Specialty-Technology	10
WisdomTree International Utilities	DBU	Specialty-Utilities	98
WisdomTree Japan High-Yielding Equity	DNL	Japan Stock	43
WisdomTree Japan SmallCap Dividend	DFJ	Japan Stock	69
WisdomTree Japan Total Dividend	DXJ	Japan Stock	41
WisdomTree LargeCap Dividend	DLN	Large Blend	246
WisdomTree Low P/E	EZY	Large Blend	22
WisdomTree MidCap Dividend	DON	Mid-Cap Blend	94
WisdomTree MidCap Earnings	EZM	Mid-Cap Blend	32
WisdomTree Pacific ex-Japan Hi-Yld Eq	DNH	Pacific/Asia ex-Japan Stk	93

Name	Ticker	Morningstar Category	Total Assets $MM
WisdomTree Pacific ex-Japan Total Div	DND	Pacific/Asia ex-Japan Stk	215
WisdomTree SmallCap Dividend	DES	Small Blend	92
WisdomTree SmallCap Earnings	EES	Small Blend	17
WisdomTree Total Dividend	DTD	Large Blend	97
WisdomTree Total Earnings	EXT	Large Blend	18

A Sampling of ETFs Currently in Filing

iShares MSCI Chile

iShares MSCI Emerging Markets Small Cap Fund

iShares MSCI Israel

Bear Stearns Current Yield Fund

Claymore/Dorchester: The Capital Markets Equities ETF

First Trust DJ STOXXSelect Dividend 30 Index Fund

IndexIQ Market Power Leaders Large Cap

IndexIQ Sustainability Leaders All Cap

MyShares ISE-CCM Homeland Security Index Fund

NETS FTSE CNBC 300 Index Fund

PowerShares DWA Emerging Markets Technical Leaders

PowerShares India Tiger

PowerShares Weekly VRDO Tax-Free

ProShares Short Consumer Goods

ProShares Short Financials

ProShares Short Healthcare

ProShares Ultra Short iBoxx $ Liquid High Yield

Rydex Inverse Consumer Staples

Rydex Dynamic Inverse Consumer Discretionary

Rydex Inverse Russell 2000 Value

StateShares California 50

StateShares Composite

SPDR S&P Europe

SPDR Leisuretime

SPDR Computer Hardware

Market Vectors—Lehman Brothers High Yield Municipal

Vanguard Mega Cap 300 Growth Index ETF

United States Heating Oil Fund

TIGERS Revenue-Weighted Large Cap Index Fund

Wilder Asian Emerging Markets

Wilder Israel

Wilder Healthy Lifestyle

WisdomTree Communications Sector

WisdomTree United Kingdom Total Dividend

AirShares EU Carbon Allowances

Glossary

actively managed fund

A fund in which a manager conducts frequent transactions, research, and forecasts.

American Depositary Receipt (ADR)

A certificate issued by a U.S. bank representing a specified number of shares in a foreign stock traded on a U.S. exchange, facilitating purchase of shares in foreign companies.

arbitrage

A concurrent purchase and sale of an asset to profit from the price differential on separate exchanges.

balanced fund

A fund containing a mix of stocks, bonds, and money market instruments in a single portfolio.

basis point

Measure of 1/100th of 1 percent, used to calculate interest rates, equity indexes, and yield of fixed-income securities.

bear market

A market in which the prices of securities are falling. A downturn of at least 15 to 20 percent in more than one index is considered to be the start of a bear market.

benchmark

The standard against which a security's performance is measured.

beta

A measure of volatility. If the beta is greater than 1, it is more volatile than the market. If it's less than 1, it is less volatile than the market. The higher the beta, the greater the potential for a high rate of return, but also of higher market risk.

blend

Also known as a hybrid fund, a category of equity mutual funds with portfolios made up of both value and growth stocks.

bull market

A market condition when securities are rising.

capital gains

Profits taxed at rates that could be lower than rates on ordinary income; the result of the sale of a capital asset.

commodity

A product used in commerce and traded on a commodity exchange.

correction

A drop of at least 10 percent in an index or market, often seen as a sign of a healthy market when part of a larger trend.

deflation

An overall decline in prices, usually caused by a drop in the supply of money or credit.

earnings per share (EPS)

A company's profit divided by the number of shares of outstanding common stock.

equal-weighted index

An index in which each company is given the same weight, so that small companies have as much impact on changes as large companies.

exchange traded fund (ETF)

A basket of stocks tracking an underlying index, commodity, bonds, or currency. ETFs are traded like stocks—daily on an exchange.

fundamentally weighted index

A type of indexing in which the stocks are chosen based on their fundamental valuations (instead of their market capitalization).

gross domestic product (GDP)

Calculated yearly, the monetary value of all finished goods and services produced within a country per year.

growth investing

Emphasis on stocks on the way up, with potential for greater-than-average returns.

hedge fund

An aggressively managed portfolio of investments, using strategies such as leverage, long, short, and derivative positions both domestically and internationally.

index

A group of securities representing a specific market or portion of a market. Among the best-known indexes are the Standard & Poor's 500 and the Dow Jones Industrial Average.

index fund

A mutual fund that tracks an index. ETFs are one example of an index fund.

inflation

The rate of change in prices for goods and services.

initial margin

The percentage of purchase price of securities an investor must place on deposit with a broker.

initial public offering (IPO)

The first sale of a stock when a private company goes public.

large-cap

Companies with a market capitalization of about $10 billion or more.

liquidity

The capability to buy or sell securities in the market without the asset's price being affected, or an asset's quick conversion to cash.

long position

Purchasing a security as the initial step in the transaction (buy, hold, sell), compared with a short position (sell, hold, buy).

margin

Money borrowed from a broker to purchase securities.

market capitalization

A company's share price times the number of shares outstanding.

market-capitalization weighted index

Weighting the stock in an index by its components' market capitalization.

market timing

A strategy in which a trader takes advantage of the different closing times of markets around the world or other factors.

microcap

Companies with a market capitalization of about $250 million or lower.

mid-cap

Companies with a market capitalization of between $1 billion and $8 billion.

minimum margin

The initial, minimum amount required to be deposited into a margin account before an investor or trader is allowed to trade on margin or to sell short.

mutual fund

Pools of money managed professionally, also called an investment company. Managers invest in stocks, bonds, options, money market instruments, and other securities.

net asset value (NAV)

Calculated daily, the total value of the portfolio of a fund minus its liabilities.

over the counter (OTC)

Any security traded somewhere other than on a formal exchange.

Over the Counter Bulletin Board (OTCBB)

A regulated electronic trading service offered by the Financial Industry Regulatory Authority (NASD), providing quotes in real time, last-sale prices, and volume information for OTC securities.

passive management

A management style in which the portfolio of a fund tracks a market index. It's the opposite of active management because it doesn't require a manager consistently doing trading and research.

Pink Sheets

A daily publication assembled by the National Quotation Bureau to provide bid and ask prices of OTC securities.

price to book ratio (P/B ratio)

A ratio comparing a stock's market value to its book value, calculated by dividing the closing price of the stock by the latest quarter's book value per share.

price-to-earnings ratio (P/E ratio)

The valuation ratio of a company's current share price compared to its per-share earnings.

price-to-earnings to growth ratio (PEG ratio)

A ratio used to determine a stock's value while also factoring in earnings growth. It's calculated as the *price-to-earnings ratio* divided by *annual EPS growth.*

price-weighted index

An index in which each stock's weight on the index is in proportion to its price per share. Therefore, stocks with a higher price are given more weight. The Dow Jones Industrial Average is an example.

quant investing

A fund that selects securities based on quantitative analysis. Managers build computer models to select investments.

return

A gain or loss of a security in a specified period, usually quoted as a percentage.

Sarbanes-Oxley Act of 2002 (SOX)

A federal law designed to protect investors from the possibility of fraudulent accounting schemes by corporations, increase SEC oversight and funding, and create an accounting oversight board.

Securities and Exchange Commission (SEC)

A government agency created under the Securities and Exchange Act of 1934, providing regulation in the securities markets.

short selling

Borrowing and then selling shares as an initial step, done on the assumption that the stock can be bought at a lower amount than the price at which the investor sold it. The sequence in a short position is sell, hold, buy, compared to that of a long position, buy, hold, sell.

small-cap

Companies with a market capitalization of between $250 million and $2 billion.

tax efficiency

A fund structured to reduce the tax liability for its shareholders.

transparency

The degree to which a security or company allows you to "know what you own."

Treasury Inflation-Protected Securities (TIPS)

A U.S. Treasury security or bond pegged to the Consumer Price Index (CPI), a nominal measure of purchasing power calculated by the U.S. Department of Labor.

turnover rate

A measurement of how often the assets in a fund are bought and sold by its managers. It is calculated by dividing the total amount of new securities bought or sold (whichever is less) by the net asset value (NAV) of the fund.

value investing

Focusing on stocks perceived to be available at bargain prices but exceptionally well managed.

variable annuity

An insurance contract guaranteeing minimum returns.

INDEX